Used

and

Rare

ALSO BY THE GOLDSTONES

Lawrence Goldstone
Rights

Nancy Goldstone
Trading Up: Surviving Success as a Woman Trader on Wall Street
Bad Business: A Novel
Mommy and the Murder
Mommy and the Money

Used and Rare

TRAVELS IN THE BOOK WORLD

LAWRENCE
AND
NANCY GOLDSTONE

St. Martin's Griffin ✸ New York

A THOMAS DUNNE BOOK.
An imprint of St. Martin's Press.

Design by Bryanna Millis

Library of Congress Cataloging-in-Publication Data

Goldstone, Lawrence.
    Used and rare: travels in the book world / Lawrence and
Nancy Goldstone.
        p.   cm.
    "A Thomas Dunne book."
    ISBN 0–312–18768–8
    1. Book collecting—New England. 2. Book collecting—
Middle Atlantic States. 3. Goldstone, Lawrence.
4. Goldstone, Nancy Bazelon. I. Goldstone, Nancy Bazelon.
II. Title.
Z987.5.U6G65   1997
002'092—dc21   96–30081

10 9 8 7 6 5 4 3

Used

and

Rare

CHAPTER 1

*W*e came to book collecting because our birthdays fall eight days apart.

When married people have birthdays that close together, a certain natural competitiveness develops. Or maybe it was just us. In any event, birthday week had degenerated into extravagant spending and a furious determination on the part of each to outdo the other that inevitably resulted in our squandering money that we could not afford on gifts the recipients didn't particularly like but, because of the cost, could not admit to disliking until months, sometimes years, later.

Finally, with the maturity that comes with advancing age, we decided to put a stop to the problem. As a result, four years ago something like the following conversation took place:

"I want you to promise me that you won't spend a lot of money on my birthday."

"Sure."

"Ohhh no. That's what you said last year and look what happened."

"What do you mean? The nightgown wasn't that expensive."

"Two hundred dollars is expensive when I only spent fifty."

"Nobody asked you to only spend fifty."

"*You* asked me to only spend fifty. You would have gotten upset if I spent more than fifty."

"Depends on what you got me."

"You never like what I get you."

"That's why I didn't want you to spend more than fifty."

"It's not fair. You have it easy. You always go second."

"Look, you knew my birthday fell eight days before yours when you married me."

"*Ten years* and eight days."

"Very funny."

"Why don't we just set a limit this year and stick to it for once?"

"Sure."

"No, I mean it. Besides, it's more creative. Unless you don't want to be creative, of course."

"I can be as creative as you."

"Great. How about forty dollars?"

"How about thirty?"

"Twenty-five."

"Twenty."

"Fif . . . okay, twenty."

"Great."

"Remember, no cheating this year. If you cheat, you lose."

"Lose? What, are we competing?"

Thus began the search for *War and Peace*.

If you want a book, the obvious place to begin is a bookstore. In Lenox, Massachusetts, where we had lived since abandoning Manhattan three years before, the local bookstore is called, conveniently enough, The Bookstore. The Bookstore ("Serving the community since last Tuesday") is owned and occasionally operated by Matthew Tannenbaum, a shaggy dog of a man who considers it a bookseller's responsibility to provide a convivial atmosphere for his customers.

"Nancy, did you hear about the two cannibals who were eating a clown?" asked Matthew. "One of the cannibals stopped for a minute and turned to the other cannibal. 'Do you taste something funny?' "

"I liked the one about the near-sighted fireman better."

Matthew looked disappointed. "So did everyone."

Jo walked up to the desk. Although she is technically an employee, Jo is actually more of a spiritual figure, a cross between an aging hippie and a schoolmarm. She has long straight gray hair, pulled back, excellent posture, a low, throaty voice, and a serious, unflappable manner. She will occasionally clasp her hands in front of her while she is speaking.

"Are you looking for anything in particular?" she asked.

In addition to the usual best-sellers and major new releases, The Bookstore stocks a larger than normal selection of obscure poetry, alternative fiction, Judaica, women's studies, Native American studies, African American studies, paranormal psychology, and organic vegetarian cookbooks. In the front, there is a rack of magazines for the intellectually serious, such as *Granta, Mother Jones,* and *The Utne Reader.* Next to the magazines, there is an extensive children's section presided over by a huge, incredibly filthy stuffed bear that every child under the age of five sticks his mouth on.

"I'm looking for *War and Peace.*"

"Certainly." Jo led the way to the paperback section at the extreme rear of the store, reached down to the bottom shelf, and produced a Penguin edition. It was so thick that it looked like a piece of a Duraflame.

"No, no. We already have a paperback. I was hoping for a hardcover. It's a birthday present for Larry."

"You're getting Larry *War and Peace* for his birthday?" interjected Matthew, who had tagged along behind us. "What's the matter? Things aren't going well at home?"

"No. We made this . . . we decided . . . forget it."

"Ah." Jo nodded sagely. "Let's check *Books in Print* then." She went back to the desk and pulled a big brown volume down from the shelf. "There's a Modern Library edition for twenty-five dollars," she said, running her finger down a column on the Tolstoy page. "We could order it for you."

"What does it look like?"

"It looks like a book," said Matthew. "What were you expecting?"

"Well, we don't have *War and Peace* in the store at the moment," Jo went on, "but we do have *David Copperfield,* if you want to get a sense of what a Modern Library book is like."

She walked across the store and plucked a small, unimpressive book from a shelf. It was flimsily bound with thin paper leaves. The print was small. It did not seem a big step up from the paperback.

"I don't think so."

"Of course." Jo nodded and consulted *Books in Print* again. "Here's another hardcover. It's a two-volume set for forty dollars."

"What does it look like? Does it *look* like a birthday present?"

"If you wrapped it, it would look like a birthday present," said Matthew.

"I mean, does it have pictures and larger type?"

"I don't know," Jo said. "I haven't seen it."

"What do you want *War and Peace* for anyway?" Matthew asked. "Why don't you get Larry a *real* classic like *Men Are from Mars, Women Are from Venus?*"

"I don't think so. Besides, Larry likes war. You should have seen him cooing over the battle maps in the Civil War book. I told him, 'If you like battles so much, read *War and Peace.* It has great battles.' But all we have is this old beat-up paperback and he said, 'The print is too small,' and I said, 'What did we get you those reading glasses for then?' and he said, 'Just because I got them doesn't mean I like to use them.' So I thought, if I got him a nice copy of *War and Peace* as a birthday present, something in hardcover with big print, he'd have to read it, and then he would have this great experience. Besides, then I'd win the bet."

"Bet?" asked Matthew. "What bet?"

"Nothing. It's a good birthday present. As long as it doesn't cost more than twenty dollars . . . or not a lot more anyway."

Jo thought for a moment. "Have you tried 'Books'?" she asked.

" 'Books'?"

"It's a used-book store in Egremont," she explained. "I'll call for you and see if they have a copy."

"A *used* book?" Buying a used book sounded worse than buying a paperback. "Used book" evoked images of smudged and dog-eared copies of college texts, *Beginning Chemistry* or some such, the relevant passages of each chapter underlined in somebody else's yellow marker.

But Jo was already on the phone to Books. Luckily, they didn't have a copy of *War and Peace* either.

Where to try next? There wasn't any point in visiting any of the other new-book stores in the area. Everyone uses the same *Books in Print*.

No, not a new book. And not a used one. That didn't seem to leave much. And then, with almost staggering naïveté, the thought of those books that they run at the beginning of Masterpiece Theater came to mind. Those looked nice. Maybe something like that. But where did one find books like those?

The Yellow Pages, of course. And there it was, right after "Book Dealers—Retail," a heretofore undiscovered category: "Book Dealers—Used & Rare." Keep it simple. Perhaps one of the listings that seemed to be just a person's name. Here was one in Alford.

On the third ring, a man picked up.

"Hello?" he said.

"Hi. My name is Nancy Goldstone. I wonder if you could help me. I'm looking for a nice hardcover edition of *War and Peace.*"

"What kind of edition?" the man asked.

"What do you mean, what kind of edition?"

"Well, do you want it in Russian?"

Russian? "No. Of course not. It's for a birthday present."

"Well, then, do you want the first American edition? The first English edition? The first French edition?"

"No. I just want a nice hardcover in English with some pictures and large type."

"You want a used book," the man said coldly. He said the word "used" as though it had an odor attached to it.

"Don't *you* sell used books?"

"No. I am an antiquarian-book dealer."

"Aren't they the same thing?"

"No."

"But I tried a used-book store and they didn't have it."

"Try the Strand," the man said, and hung up.

The Strand, on Fourth Avenue and Eleventh Street in New York City, is perhaps the largest and most well-known used-book store in the country. It has as much floor space as an aircraft hangar and, as its advertising states, "over one million books."

From Lenox to lower Manhattan is a long-distance phone call, but it seemed worth the expense. Someone at the Strand answered the phone on the third ring, listened politely to the query, said, "Could you please hold for a moment?" and then never came back.

That left Clarence.

Clarence was Clarence Wolf, who lived with his wife, Ruth, in a two-bedroom high-rise apartment just off Lake Shore Drive in Chicago, featuring huge picture windows that provided a spectacular view of Lincoln Park, downtown Chicago, and Lake Michigan. The apartment was filled with beautiful antiques, lovely paintings, and, most significantly, books. Hundreds of books. Clarence had been collecting books for over sixty years.

Clarence was ninety-three.

Age, however, had not slowed him a whit. He was intelligent, articulate, and erudite. He read *Intellectual* magazine. Clarence loved to talk about books. Clarence loved to talk about Churchill. He loved to talk about marriage and the railroads. However, in a family that thought nothing of engaging in minutely detailed discussions of their golf game, hole by hole, stroke by stroke, no one really listened.

"Hello, Nancy," he said when Ruth called him to the telephone. "This is Clarence Wolf. How's my granddaughter?"

The quest was explained.

"War and Peace? Wonderful, Nancy. Wonderful. Couldn't be better," he said. "You know, *War and Peace* is on Professor Robert Maynard Hutchins list of the ten greatest books of all time. I have the article in the *Chicago Tribune* right here. 'Professor Hutchins List of the Ten Greatest Books of All Time to Serve as Cornerstone for American Role in World Government.' He lists Plato, Aristotle, Homer, St. Augustine, St. Thomas Aquinas, Dante, Tolstoy—that's the one you're interested in, *War and Peace*—Pascal, Shakespeare, and Thucydides. I don't know what the date is on this—it doesn't say— but it was when we were interested in world government. Must be at least twenty-five years ago. But it's a very good list. I don't want to bore you, but I was just reading Churchill this morning, you know, some people think it is all right to go out and play golf every morning, and I don't want to criticize, I don't have any argument with golf, but to me, there's nothing finer than getting dressed in a nice suit in the morning, you know, Dr. Samuel Johnson said that clothes make the man, and I'm not sure but I think he's right, that's why I wear a suit every morning, and I know I've said this a thousand times, but some people think it's all right to wear shorts or not to shower before sitting down to breakfast and I'm not saying they're wrong, but, I know you'll appreciate this, Nancy, there's nothing more wonderful than getting up in the morning and getting clean and putting on a dress shirt, a silk tie, a well-made suit and then sitting down to a nice breakfast, not too much, just some coffee and orange juice and buttered toast, perhaps an egg, and then, afterward, sitting down with Winston Churchill, and as you know, I make notes on what I want to read every morning, and I hope I'm not boring you with this, Nancy, but when I make the notes it makes me feel like I'm having a conversation with Churchill. Now let me see, you wanted to know where to obtain a copy of *War and Peace* . . ."

"Yes. Do you know where I might find one? I was hoping to get a nice copy."

"A nice copy," he repeated, turning it over in his head. "Well, you could try Maggs Brothers. They're very fine book dealers in London. Very fine. They carry only the very best works. I bought one of my first books from Maggs. That was in . . . I remember how wonderful it was to get their first catalogue. I've been getting their catalogue for a number of years now. I bought my *Alice in Wonderland* from them. Beautiful book. Not a first, but an early edition, very finely bound. If you write to Maggs, tell them that Clarence Wolf recommended you and I'm sure they'll send you a catalogue."

It was lovely of him to take the time but London seemed a little far.

"Well, all right. Thank you, Clarence. Let me look into that. I'll talk to you again soon."

Within forty-five seconds, the phone rang.

"Hello?"

"Hello, Nancy, it's Clarence Wolf."

"Why, hello, Clarence. Is something—"

"I thought of something else. If Maggs doesn't have it, you might try William Reese. I have one of their catalogues right here. I can mail it to you, if you'd like."

"Does it have *War and Peace*?"

"No, no, I don't think so, but it's a wonderful catalogue. You know, you're going to find that this is a marvelous adventure you've started on. You'll forgive my going on like this, but the accumulation of a library is a wonderful occupation. I've devoted much of my life to this pleasure of mine. I read an hour or so every day. There is no substitute for great books. My books are like having some of the greatest minds in history in my home with me. I can pick up Shakespeare or Churchill or Dickens anytime I want."

"Well, thank you, Clarence, I'll look into it."

"Shall I send you the William Reese catalogue?"

"Sure. Thank you."

A minute later the phone rang again.

"Hello?"

"Hello, Nancy. This is Clarence Wolf."

"Hello, Clarence."

"I thought of something else. If you're going to do this, you should do a little reading. If I were you, I'd pick up *The Amenities of Book-Collecting* by A. Edward Newton."

"Thank you, Clarence. I will."

"I hope I didn't talk too much. And don't hesitate to call me if you need any more advice." He paused. "I'm also interested in fine wines, you know."

The Amenities of Book-Collecting turned out to be a small, decrepit volume sitting at the very back of the nonfiction stacks in the Lenox library. Only seven other people had ever checked it out. The most recent was twenty years ago. The first was in 1940.

First published in 1918, *The Amenities of Book-Collecting* was a wildly popular work that had at least eight to ten printings over fifteen years. Book collecting was all the rage back then and Newton rode the crest. While full of interesting information, *Amenities* seemed to lack current relevance. It spoke of Shelley, Keats, Lamb, and Oscar Wilde as "modern" authors. The prices of books were reported with great care—but they were the prices of 1918. Newton wrote loving and detailed descriptions of bookshops and booksellers who had been dead for fifty years.

Not just the subject matter was dated. The following is typical of Newton's prose:

> If you would know the delight of book collecting, begin with something else, I care not what. Book collecting has all the advantages of other hobbies without their drawbacks. The pleasure of acquisition is common to all—that's where the sport lies; but the strain of the possession of books is almost nothing: a tight, dry closet will serve to house them, if need be.
>
> It is not so with flowers. They are a constant care. Someone once wrote a poem about "old books and fresh flowers." It lilted along very nicely; but I remark that

books stay old, indeed get older, and flowers do not stay fresh: a little too much rain, a little too much sun, and it is over.

There was no mention whatever of *War and Peace*.

A few days later, a parcel arrived in the mail from Clarence and Ruth. It contained two book catalogues and a scrawled letter from Clarence containing a list of other books that he thought would be useful to someone who intended to become a book collector. The biography of somebody called Rosenbach headed the list.

One of the catalogues was from William Reese and the other was from Maggs Brothers, the two book dealers he had mentioned on the telephone. The Maggs Brothers catalogue was larger. It had a glossy cover and was filled with illustrations. It was dated 1993 and numbered 1157.

Each item in the Maggs catalogue was described in detail and annotated with as much as a page of explanatory notes. It was, in itself, an interesting read. There was a two-volume, privately printed, 1726 edition of *Gulliver's Travels,* signed photographs of Queen Victoria, works by Shaw, E. M. Forster, and T. S. Eliot and a 1755 Samuel Johnson *Dictionary of the English Language.* Perhaps the most unusual item was a document signed by Ferdinand of Aragon and Isabella of Castile (of the Christopher Columbus Ferdinand and Isabella), in which they are making arrangements for their daughter Juana to sail to Flanders to rejoin her husband, Philip the Fair. Maggs added the following:

> A document of historic interest. The tragic Princess Juana was the heiress to the thrones of both her parents after the deaths of her brother and elder sister. A sullen, rather plain girl, she was married in 1496 to the very handsome Philip the Fair, who was governing Flanders for his father, the Hapsburg Emperor Maximilian I. She fell passionately in love with her husband, who was completely indifferent

to her, and her grief and despair drove her into actual insanity after a few years. After 1502 she was generally known as Juana la Loca—Juana the Mad. She returned to Flanders in the Spring of 1504 after a lengthy visit to her parents; the elaborate preparations are indicated in the present document. Shortly after her return she physically attacked her husband's mistress in the presence of the whole court and the foreign ambassadors and cut off her hair. Philip, beside himself with rage, publicly cursed and repudiated her. The scandal reverberated throughout Europe, making Isabella ill from grief and shame. Unhappiness over her daughter probably accelerated Isabella's death in November, 1504, nine months after the date of this document. Juana inherited the throne of Castile, with her father Ferdinand as regent because of her insanity. There were frequent disputes between Ferdinand and his son-in-law Philip, and Philip's early death in 1506 gave rise to rumours that Ferdinand had had him poisoned. The son of the tragic marriage of Juana and Philip became the brilliant Holy Roman Emperor and King of Spain, Charles V.

Lucky for Columbus that he left when he did.

Fascinating stuff, but Maggs was going to be no help in finding a twenty-dollar copy of *War and Peace,* or a twenty-dollar anything for that matter, except perhaps the catalogue itself. There didn't seem to be anything *in* the Maggs catalogue that didn't end in either two or three zeroes and their prices were in pounds. The Ferdinand and Isabella document, for example, was listed at £2,400.

The search for *War and Peace* had by this time assumed the proportions of a holy quest. There was nothing to do but press on and take one last shot at the Yellow Pages. Back to "Book Dealers—Used & Rare," where one used-book store all the way in Sheffield had paid for a slightly larger ad.

"Do you have a nice hardcover edition of *War and Peace*?"

"Let me see," said the woman who answered the phone. "Can you hold a moment?"

Uh-oh.

But the woman was back on the line in a few seconds. "Yes," she said.

"You *do?*"

"Yes."

"What does it look like?"

"It's a Heritage edition in very good condition."

"Does it have pictures?"

"Illustrations, you mean? Yes. And the Maude translation as well."

"What's the Maude translation?"

"Louise and Aylmer Maude. They devoted their lives to translating Tolstoy's works. They even went to Russia and spent an extended period visiting Tolstoy on his estate south of Moscow. Aylmer wrote a biography of Tolstoy as well. The Maude translation is considered definitive."

"Is the print small?"

"Oh, no. It's quite nice. It has maps of the major battles, fold-out color illustrations, and its own slipcase . . ."

"How much is it?"

"Ten dollars."

"I'll take it."

"Will you be coming in, or shall I mail it to you?" asked the woman.

"Happy birthday!"

"What is it?"

"It's your present. Under twen-ty dolll-lars."

Pause. Flurried unwrapping. "It's *War and Peace.*"

"I know. I got it for you."

"Uh—great. Thank you."

"The print's not too small, is it?"

"What do I care how big the print is?"

"Oh, right. The illustrations are nice, too. And see? There are maps of the battlefields . . ."

"Oh yeah? Let me see." Pause. "This is about Napoléon's attacking Russia, isn't it?"

"Among other things. It's the Maude translation, too."

"What's the Maude translation?"

"Louise and Aylmer Maude. They spent their lives translating Tolstoy. They even went to Russia to visit him and wrote a biography. The Maude translation is considered definitive."

"All right, all right. Thanks a lot. I'll read it."

For the next three weeks, we talked about *War and Peace*.

"Wow. Did you know that all the major figures that Tolstoy wrote about actually existed? This guy Kutuzov is unbelievable."

"Which one is Kutuzov?"

"Which one is Kutuzov? He's the general! The one who only had one eye! The one who saved the Russian army by retreating out of Moscow! I thought you said you read this book."

"I liked the parties."

"You didn't read the battles at all?"

"I kind of skimmed them."

"You've got no taste. Well, all the famous people at the parties were real, too."

"Like who?"

"Oh, there was that actress and Madame de Staël . . . all the czar's relatives . . . everybody but the main characters were real people."

"How did you find all this out?"

"It's in the notes. The notes are almost better than the book. Didn't you read the notes either?"

"There weren't any notes in the paperback."

"You're kidding. How could you enjoy the book without the notes?"

"I liked the love story. I didn't care if it was real."

"I can't believe you. Remember when they went for the sleigh ride? How cold it was? You know what the notes said? It was thirty below! The nobility used to do that in Russia. Go sleigh riding at night when it was thirty below!"

"Really."

"And did you know that before Borodino, the biggest battle in the whole campaign, Napoléon put off a strategy conference so that he could talk to the artist he had dragged along with him and check the progress on a portrait of his son that he had commissioned and then sat there and made minute corrections to what the guy had done while all his generals sat around with their thumbs up their ass?"

"Fascinating."

"I can't believe you never read this stuff. Did you know that Tolstoy based some of the worst characters in the book on members of his own family?"

"I guess you really like the book then."

"Of cour . . . didn't you like what I got you?"

"Sure, honey. The bath brush was great."

CHAPTER 2

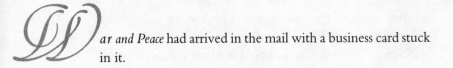*ar and Peace* had arrived in the mail with a business card stuck in it.

BERKSHIRE BOOK COMPANY
David and Esther Kininmonth
Main Street, Sheffield

So, one beautiful Saturday afternoon in early fall, we got in the car and headed down to Sheffield.

Berkshire County forms a slightly truncated rectangle at the western end of Massachusetts. It is forty miles by twenty, with the longer side running north to south and borders Vermont to the north, New York to the west, and Connecticut to the south. It is divided by residents into thirds. "South County" runs from the Connecticut border north to Great Barrington, "Mid-County" from Stockbridge through Pittsfield to Lanesborough, and "North County" up through Williamstown to the Vermont border.

Sheffield is the southernmost town in South County, about a half-hour drive from Lenox. Sheffield is much less densely populated than Lenox and is inhabited principally by second-home owners, antique dealers, and mosquitoes (it's on a floodplain). It used to have the oldest covered bridge in Massachusetts but a couple of years ago three local kids burned it down.

We drove south through Great Barrington and on into Sheffield, keeping a lookout for the Berkshire Book Company. Main Street is actually Route 7, the main north-south connector road for the county. Most of Route 7 is commercial but, in Sheffield, virtually all the shops and dealers were housed in the rambling old colonials that people used to live in before the Berkshires discovered the New York tourist trade. We drove through the one-hundred-yard town center, past the BRIDGE CLOSED sign, and on south without spotting Berkshire Book Company. The buildings began to become more irregularly spaced and we were just about to give up, thinking we'd passed it, when we saw a small red, white, and blue sign that read BERKSHIRE BOOK COMPANY, with a smaller sign hanging underneath that said OPEN. We slammed on the brakes, ignored the honking horn behind us, and churned into a gravel driveway.

On the right was a house, once again a charming, green-shuttered-white-clapboard-New-England-colonial. To the left was a grim, red outbuilding. In a previous incarnation, it appeared to have housed either a car or a hay wagon. Maybe a cow. Pasted to a small glass window on the door was a little sign that read BERKSHIRE BOOK COMPANY. We didn't know exactly what we'd been expecting, but whatever it was, it wasn't this.

The red building maintained its image on the inside as well. The floorboards were creaky, the lighting inadequate. It seemed to be both too hot and too cold at the same time. Bagpipe music was playing from a tinny speaker somewhere. There was the hint of an odd odor in the air, somewhere between an old, musty closet and fertilizer.

Everywhere we looked, we saw books. Every available inch of wall space was covered with shelves that were crammed full of books. Except for a minimal amount of aisle space, the floor was covered with books as well. Right by the door there was a tiny desk (it would probably have been a normal-size desk if there hadn't been so many books on it) with an adding machine and a tin cash drawer shoved off to one side. On the floor were stacks of books two feet tall that made the desk look like a fort. A pleasant-looking man of about fifty with straight brown hair that fell forward over his forehead, wearing a short-sleeve, plaid, pastel button-down shirt, sat at the desk, leafing through, what else, a book. He glanced up and smiled as we walked in.

"Goo'dye," he said amiably, sounding like an educated Paul Hogan.

We stood just inside the door for a moment, unable to decide which way to go. We were standing in what just one month before we would have dismissed as a junk shop, yet we found ourselves suddenly as silent and respectful as if we had just walked into a cathedral. It was an odd reaction. The vast majority of these books, on first perusal, weren't even attractive. Certainly not new and shiny. In fact, neither new *nor* shiny.

"Is there something I moight help you with?" the man behind the desk asked. The accent was not quite Australian either.

"Uh, no. We just want to look around, if that's all right."

"Help yourself." The man nodded pleasantly and once again returned to his leafing.

We discovered immediately that browsing at Berkshire Book Company was not like browsing in any bookstore we had ever been in before. When we browsed through the literature section of a new-book store, even one of the new chain mega-stores, we were at least noddingly familiar with the names of the authors they kept in stock. This stock list is obviously heavily weighted toward modern novels, books assigned in college literature courses, and whichever titles Merchant and Ivory or Emma Thompson happen to be making a film of.

Here, the literature section alone occupied three of the shop's four walls in the main room on the first floor, going around like a big U, filled with rows and rows of books by authors we had never heard of. Who, for example, was George Ade? Was George Lincoln a relative of Abraham's? What about Josephine Tey? Was that Sterling Hayden, the actor?

It got even more complicated. There was the type of edition to consider. This had never been a problem before. A new-book store usually carries only one edition of the book you want and, for all but new releases, that would be a paperback. You either bought it or you didn't.

Here everything was in hardcover and there were often two or three editions to chose from. We could see, for example, that all *War and Peace*s were not created equal. Was our single-volume Heritage *War and Peace* for ten dollars better or worse than the fifteen-dollar two-volume Heritage edition that was on the shelf now? And why was the 1942 Simon and Schuster Inner Sanctum edition (nice dust jacket, Maude translation, great maps, no illustrations, no notes) priced at twenty dollars while an older Modern Library edition (better quality than the current Modern Library edition, inferior translation, no maps, no illustrations, no notes) was selling for nine-fifty?

We wandered around the store trying to figure out how things worked here. Eventually, we meandered on back to the desk.

The pleasant-looking man looked up again. "Foind everything you were looking for?" he asked.

"Do you have a Heritage Press edition of *The Great Gatsby*?" Before we had gotten into the car, we had made a mental list of books that might be nice to have around the house. We had noticed a couple of days before that our paperback of *Gatsby* was falling apart.

The man considered. "I down't think there is one," he said, "but let's gow and tyke a look."

He led us to a bookcase near the far wall that we had missed. There were about fifty volumes from Heritage Press in a section labeled PRIVATE PRESSES. Next to them were Franklin Press and Easton Press. We recognized the Easton *Moby-Dick* from the ads in *Smithsonian*. It was their teaser. Nine dollars and ninety-five cents for *Moby-Dick,* then some indeterminate number of additional books at forty dollars a pop. They seemed very handsome. We had once considered enrolling.

"Oh, *Moby-Dick.*"

"Yes," noted the man. "The *leatherbounds.*" He said "leather-bounds" the way Harold Bloom might say "Judith Krantz."

Okay, what was wrong with the "leatherbounds?" It was clear from his tone that this was not a subjective issue. All those people who had responded to the ads in *Smithsonian* had obviously committed an expensive blunder.

But why? We stared at the books. There didn't *seem* to be anything wrong with them. They were finely bound, the leather looked expensive, the quality of the paper was good, it had gilt edging, and there was one of those soft little ribbons to keep your place with. Were they too gaudy? Was the gold embossing overdone? Was this like seeing a polyurethaned sideboard in an antique shop?

"What's wrong with the leatherbounds?"

"Ow, there's nothing wrong with them," the man said dismissively. "People bring them in here all the toime. They spend a couple of thowsand dollahs on them to build up a loibrary then decide they don't loike them anymore and bring them in expecting to recoup their investment. They get very upset when they foind out that they're pretty much worthless. There's just no demand. A lot of dealers wown't tyke them at all."

"Oh." We looked at each other. "What about the Heritage editions?"

"Oh, they're qwoit noice," he replied, his tone changing. "It's an offshoot of the Limited Editions Club, y'know."

"What's the Limited Editions Club?"

"The Limited Editions Club was started by George Macy," he said, pronouncing it "Mycy." "It was in the lyte twenties, I believe, before the stock market crash. Mycy took books he thought people wanted in their loibraries and commissioned a proivate printer to produce a qwoite handsome printed and bownd edition in a very limited run. Everything was first-ryte. The best printer, the best pyper." He paused for breath and to see if we were still interested. "He commissioned the best ahtists of the toime to provide the illustrytions. He got Matisse for *Ulysses* and Norman Rockwell for Mark Twyne.

He even got Picasso to do *Lysistrata*. The books were soigned and then sowld to collectors." He smiled. It was a stiff little smile. We couldn't tell if he was trying not to smile and couldn't help himself or trying to smile and not quite being able to get it out all the way. "The limitytions on the run were supposed to droive up the proice.

"The Heritage Press editions used the syme text and illustrytions as the Limited Editions version but were bownd and printed commercially. Also, they weren't soigned, of course, and were issued from a much lahger run for a more general audience." He squinted at the bookcase in front of him and plucked a volume from the shelf. It contained both H. G. Wells's *War of the Worlds* and *Time Machine*. "They're qwoite nice, actually," he repeated, taking the book out of its slipcase and looking it over. He did not seem to hold the book as much as caress it.

"In this one, the two works are bound dos-à-dos, back to back. If a dos-à-dos book is placed flat on a tyble, it is always fyce up." He showed us. "It's always fyce down, too, of course," he added. Then he pulled a small folded piece of pyper . . . uh, paper, from the slip-case.

"Each Heritage selection was produced with a little newsletter called *The Sandglass,* which talks about the book and the author and the illustrytor." He showed us the newsletter. It was entitled *Of Martians and Morlocks.*

"See here," he said, pointing. "Wells was only twenty-noine when *The Toime Machine* came out . . ."

"We'll take it."

"I down't think you'll be disappointed," said the man. "Needless to sye, the Heritage editions are substantially cheaper than the Limited Editions Club books. They were about forty dollars new, I believe. A perfectly serviceable library can be stocked exclusively from used Heritage editions at no more than ten, twenty, or, at most, twenty-five dollahs per book." He checked inside the front cover. "This one is ten dollahs."

We looked through the rest of the bookcase and withdrew a copy of Theodore Dreiser's *Sister Carrie*.

"That's another good one," said the man, pointing to the Dreiser. "Reginald Marsh did the illustrytions."

We nodded. We had no idea who Reginald Marsh was.

We trooped back through the cramped aisle to the desk. We watched as the man added up our purchases and put the books in a plain brown paper bag.

"Too bad they're not Limited Editions," we said.

"Actually," said the man, handing us the bag, "unless you were lucky enough to get a soigned *Ulysses,* things didn't work out that well. A lot of the Limited Editions aren't even worth what people pyde for them originally."

"Really."

"Oh, yes, that's the book business. You never know. By the wye, the nyme's Dyve Kininmonth." He put out his hand.

"Larry and Nancy Goldstone."

We all shook hands. David's brow furrowed. Then he brightened. "Oh, roight," he said. "How'd you loike the *War and Peace?*"

We went home and read *The War of the Worlds* and *The Time Machine;* we reread *Sister Carrie.* We liked the feel of our new books; we liked the printing; we liked reading *The Sandglass.* We liked Reginald Marsh's illustrations so much that we went to the library and looked him up. He turned out to be a well-known artist and illustrator of the twenties and thirties who worked for *Harpers* and the *New Yorker,* among others, and whose paintings of revelers at Coney Island and vagrants on the Bowery are considered among the best of the period.

Two weeks later we were back at the Berkshire Book Company.

David was at the desk again when we walked in. "Hello," he said, smiling. "Good to see you again. Back for more Heritage?"

"Do you have *The Great Gatsby* at all?"

"*Gatsby* again, huh?" David said. "In hahdcover, I take it."

"Yes." We weren't interested in paperbacks anymore.

"I down't think so," said David, coming out from behind the

desk and heading to the "F's" in the literature section. "They're pretty hahd to come by." He perused the Fitzgeralds. *Tender Is the Night* was there, *This Side of Paradise*, *The Last Tycoon*, but no *Gatsby*. "I didn't think so," he said.

"What about *Dracula?*"

" 'Fryde not."

"The Grapes of Wrath?"

"Don't think so."

Nor did he have *The Hamlet, Daisy Miller,* or anything by B. Traven.

"What about *The Guns of August?*" we asked, moving to non-fiction.

"We sowld one Thursday," David replied. "Noice copy, too."

We didn't remember having seen *The Guns of August* the last time we were there. "Was it here two weeks ago?"

"No," said David. "We got it in two dyes before we sowld it. Things come in and out of here all the toime."

"Oh." It hadn't occurred to us that we could miss both the arrival and irrevocable departure of a book we wanted. That never happens at a new-book store. If they are sold out of something you want, they simply order you another one.

David noticed our disappointment. "I do have another Bahbara Tuchman, though," he said. "It cyme in at the syme toime."

"Which one?"

"Stilwell and the American Experience in Choina."

"Really?"

Stilwell is a brilliantly written account of a clash of cultures, one of which happens to be ours. "Vinegar Joe" Stilwell was a hard-bitten American general, deeply moral and fabulously courageous (by American standards) who was assigned to supply and support the deeply immoral and fabulously opportunistic (by American standards) Chaing Kai-shek during the Japanese occupation of China in World War II. It was Barbara Tuchman's other Pulitzer Prize winner. Like *The Guns of August*, we had it in paperback but it was in terrible condition. Although we hadn't thought about it until David mentioned it, it would be great to have a hardcover copy of *Stilwell* in the house.

"Would you loike to see it? It's not even on the shelf yet."

David led us across the floor to the stairway that led to the second floor where the nonfiction was kept. There it was, in a pile on the top step, *Stilwell and the American Experience in China.* We eagerly picked it up and looked inside the cover. Ten dollars.

"It's a book club edition, though," David added.

"Does that matter?"

"Didn't used to," he said. "In the old dyes, the book clubs would use the same plytes as the publisher and print their editions on first-class quality pyper and do the syme with the boinding. Now though, the pyper is flimsier and the boindings are not particularly good, so book club editions are worth a lot less than publishers' editions. Collectors won't touch them.

"Here," he said, picking up another book from the stack. "This is a regular tryde edition. Feel the difference in the pyper."

We opened each volume and did as David suggested. The paper in the trade edition was of noticeably better quality.

"It's the syme with the boindings. If you don't tyke special care with book club editions, the boindings will crack on you."

"So are you saying we shouldn't buy book club editions?"

"No, no. Not at all," David replied. "We sell them all the toime. Sometoimes you can only get a book club edition of a book you want. Besides, they're a lot cheaper . . . should be anywye. Just myke sure you're not pying for a tryde edition and getting a book club edition."

"How can you tell? By the paper?"

"Most toimes," David replied. "But there are other wyes, too. Sometoimes it says 'Book Club Edition' on the inside of the dust jacket or on the copyright page . . ."

"That sounds easy."

"But usually not."

"Oh."

"Mostly though, book club editions don't have a proice on the dust jacket . . . but then the dust jackets are often clipped to tyke the proice off anywye."

"Oh."

"The best wye is like this . . ." David took the dust jacket off *Stilwell* and pointed to the bottom of the back cover, near the spine.

"See that?" he said. There was a small imprint, a little circle pressed into the cover. "All the book club editions have an imprint loike this. Sometoimes it's a circle or a square, sometoimes a little figure. But if you see one, it's a book club edition for sure."

We nodded. "How long have you been in this business?"

He laughed. "Just a couple of years. I was a tryde representative in the New Zealand Foreign Service for most of moy career. Esthah was the one with the books. She would never throw anything out. My last assignment was in Washington, and we had a four-story house. But it was so crowded with books there almost wasn't room for us. One dye I counted and we had six hundred boxes of books. So I said to her, 'Esthah, either we get rid of some of these boxes or I tyke early retirement and we open a bookstore.' "

"Do you like it?"

"Ow, yes. It's quoite noice having a place to put all the books."

On our third visit to the Berkshire Book Company we went in looking for H. P. Lovecraft.

H. P. (for Howard Phillips) Lovecraft is one of the masters of the macabre. He was born in 1890 and lived most of his life in Providence, Rhode Island. As a child he was an invalid, confined to the home of his well-to-do grandfather where he passed the time by reading gothic fiction. Both of his parents died insane. He grew up to be extremely tall, exceptionally ugly, and cadaverously pale. He only went out at night, walking the streets of Providence dressed in a long coat, slouch hat, and cape.

He set much of his work in parallel netherworlds populated by hideous part-human creatures. He was particularly partial to subterranean New England and wrote such masterpieces of horror as *The Rats in the Walls, In the Vault,* and *The Thing on the Doorstep*. Despite the acclaim he received after his death in 1937, Lovecraft died penniless and convinced he had been a failure. He was anything but. Any writer of the genre who has come since, up to and including Stephen King, owes—and will acknowledge—the extreme influence that Lovecraft had on his or her work.

We didn't know whether Lovecraft would be filed under literature, mystery, or horror so, before looking around blindly, we decided to ask. Dyvid wasn't manning the fort that day. Instead, a jolly-looking, animated woman in her fifties with a long, single, waist-length, salt-and-pepper braid that itself looked as if it had been lifted from a Pearl Buck novel, smiled expectantly as we walked in. This, we surmised, getting the hang of it, was Esther of the six hundred boxes of books.

"Do you have any H. P. Lovecraft in hardcover?"

The woman hesitated. "We might have one." She stood up, came out from behind the barricade, and started picking her way through one of the aisles, all the while looking back at us and smiling and talking. "Whenever we get one, it goes right away. People collect H. P. Lovecraft, even the reprints."

"What do you mean, the reprints?"

"Well, Lovecraft had just started becoming a cult figure when he died. But there was still no real demand for his work. In fact, he had only been published in cheap magazines and never had a collection of stories in book form until 1936, which was the year before he died." She spoke as if going to look for H. P. Lovecraft was the thing she had been waiting to do all day. "It was a publisher called Visionary Press, interestingly enough . . . and even then only a couple of hundred copies were printed. The only people who would take a chance on Lovecraft stories after that were two men named Donald Wandrei and August Derleth . . . Derleth was a writer of some note himself . . . who started a press called Arkham House in their home town of Sauk City, Wisconsin, in 1939 with a Lovecraft collection called *The Outsider and Others*. They subsequently published a number of other collections of his work. Arkham House, mostly because of Lovecraft, has since gone on to become one of the most influential publishers of horror and fantasy fiction." She chuckled. "Derleth and Wandrei made a potful of money in the bargain."

"That sounds great. Do you have any of those? The Arkham House editions?"

"Heavens, no," she said, turning around in surprise. "I've heard of Lovecraft firsts going for up to ten thousand dollars."

Ten thousand dollars? For H. P. Lovecraft? Obviously, we had heard of the Gutenberg Bible and knew that it went for millions, and Shakespeare was certainly up there, too, and then there was that Maggs catalogue, but a cult writer of horror stories who had died virtually unpublished in 1937, to have one of *his* books go for ten thousand dollars . . . the entire world of used books was transformed in that instant.

"You're kidding!"

"Indeed not." She shook her head emphatically. "The early collections are quite rare, you know," she said. "Of the ones that were published, many were allowed to fall into disrepair or were lost or destroyed. There is intense demand for those remaining, particularly if they happen to be in excellent condition. That makes all the difference, you know. Some of the other collections are not nearly so expensive.

"Ooh, you're in luck," she said, stopping in front of one of the shelves. "This one is still here."

She took a worn volume without a dust jacket off the shelf. It was called *Best Supernatural Stories of H. P. Lovecraft.*

"This is a World Press reprint of an earlier Arkham House edition," she said.

"Is a reprint a second edition?"

"No. A second edition is the second printing of a book by the original publisher. It is usually identical, or almost identical, to the first edition. A reprint is printed sometime after the original edition by a reprint publisher who has bought the rights from the original publisher and produces a cheaper edition for the mass market."

We tentatively opened the cover. It cost $7.50.

"We'll take it."

"Lovely. By the way," the woman continued, "have you ever tried Sheridan Le Fanu? He was earlier than Lovecraft. He wrote at the end of the nineteenth century. 'Green Tea' is his most famous story. It's quite good." She moved a little bit down the shelves and pulled out another volume. It was also $7.50. "If you want, you can take this and, if you don't like it, just return it and we'll give you your money back."

"Thank you." We had never been offered a money-back guarantee on a book before.

"Oh, you're very welcome," she replied. "By the way, I'm Esther Kininmonth."

"Larry and Nancy Goldstone."

"Oh, so *you're* the Goldstones," she said. "How did you like the *War and Peace*?"

CHAPTER 3

By late November, we had a tiny section on our shelves devoted to Berkshire Book Company purchases. We had added a number of Heritage volumes, such as Boswell's *Life of Johnson, The Mysterious Island* by Jules Verne, and *The Diary of Samuel Pepys.* We had also purchased a nice, illustrated *Huckleberry Finn* for four dollars and *Tom Sawyer* for five. We had even found *Mr. Bridge,* by Evan S. Connell, one of our favorites, grabbing it from the New Acquisitions section as soon as we walked in the door. It had read "1st" on the inside cover and commanded the heady price of fifteen dollars. (We were hoping to find *Mrs. Bridge* as well but it wasn't there. We thought it curious at the time that someone would have one without the other.)

Since David and Esther obviously couldn't have *everything,* we decided to branch out and visit the other used-book stores in the area. Maybe one of them had a nice, used *Great Gatsby* or *Mrs. Bridge* or *Guns of August.* We looked in the Yellow Pages again and saw that, in Berkshire County, there were twenty-one separate listings under "Book Dealers—Used & Rare." Even avoiding anything with "rare" in the title—strongly suspecting that "rare" was synonymous with "expensive"—there were still over fifteen to chose from.

We decided to start with "Books Bruce & Sue Gventer" on Route 23 in South Egremont, which was about a thirty-minute drive from our house. It was the place that Jo at The Bookstore in Lenox had first called to ask about a used *War and Peace*. Winter had set in early (as always) and exploring a used-book store seemed like a cozy thing to do on a cold, gray Saturday afternoon.

When we got to South Egremont, we realized that we had passed the sign out in front—BOOKS, it read—many times before, and had often wondered about it but had always concluded that it must be just a regular bookstore.

We followed the arrows from Route 23 and, just down a dirt road, we turned into a curving dirt driveway. "Books Bruce & Sue Gventer" was housed in an outbuilding in back of another old colonial, but this outbuilding made Berkshire Book Company's outbuilding look like one of those luxury condominiums they pitch to the Tanglewood crowd. Taped to the glass pane on the old, cracked door, just above the peeling paint, was a little sign that read BOOKS BRUCE & SUE GVENTER. WINTER HOURS. SATURDAY AND SUNDAY. 10–5. OTHER TIMES BY APPOINTMENT ONLY. There was no sign of life anywhere but this *was* Saturday and it was between ten and five (we assumed the sign referred to daylight hours) so we tried the door. Sure enough, it was open.

We paused just inside. The room was pretty much what you'd expect from the outside, but everything was a little off. The floors were swayed, the walls were curved, and the shelves were bowed. There didn't seem to be a right angle in the entire place. But "Books" was packed with books. It was also completely devoid of human life.

It took us very little time to figure out why no one else was there. "Books Bruce & Sue Gventer" was unheated. There was a small space heater near the desk at the front whose coils were glowing an encouraging bright orange but whose effective range seemed to reach only as far as the empty chair behind the desk, about six inches away. We were trying to decide if this store operated on the honor system or if we had read the sign wrong when a heretofore unnoticed back door opened and a man walked through. We recognized him. We had often seen him at John Andrews, a restaurant just across the road and one of our favorite places to eat in the Berkshires. John Andrews isn't exactly cheap and we had often wondered who the bald, disheveled man with the chest-length beard, flannel shirt, and ratty jeans was. Now we knew. He was Bruce Gventer.

To greet his customers, Bruce wore a heavy winter coat, gloves, hat, and scarf, although the scarf was almost completely obscured by the beard. He nodded to us and immediately made for the space heater.

Once again, there were so many books stuffed into the space that it was difficult to walk through. The store's "new acquisition" section consisted of four or five three-foot-high piles of books of all descriptions at the front of the store. Right on top of one of the piles were two volumes of *Best American Short Stories*.

As we reached for them, Bruce reproached us.

"Don't touch those," he said sharply. "They're not priced yet."

"Oh," we said weakly and put them back. "Uh—where's the literature section?"

He pointed to the rear of the shop. "It might be a little cold back there," he said.

We started down the aisle, stamping our feet occasionally to make sure the blood was still circulating. When we got to the literature section, we could also see that at "Books Bruce & Sue Gventer," they were not particularly concerned with fiction. Unlike the literature section at Berkshire Book Company, which occupied three full walls, the literature section here was crammed into a small corner and consisted of either books that had been published within the last two or three years or beat-up copies of older books, few of which we had ever heard of. While the filing was theoretically alphabetical, in practical terms it could best be described as haphazard. We decided to move on.

The local history section, on the other hand, was fascinating and contained well-kept and scrupulously filed books, some of which were well over one hundred years old. The art and architecture sections were also excellent, as was world history, women's studies, and the other social sciences (although, once again, no *Guns of August*). Obviously, the stock at used-book stores, like pets, tended to reflect the personalities of their owners. We surmised that Bruce Gventer was a nonfiction kind of guy.

We were just rounding the corner on our way out, when we saw a Heritage Press section. As we were once again nearing the space heater, we were willing to take a look. But Heritage obviously wasn't Bruce's thing either. The selection, while reasonably large, was not especially interesting and the books were often in poor condition.

But on the shelf next to Heritage was Trollope. A lot of Trollope. A set.

Anthony Trollope was a Victorian writer who wove long, intricate, scathingly satiric tales of political intrigue, religion, and love, filled with eccentric and flamboyant characters. Trollope's *Parliamentary Novels* were a cross between *Primary Colors* and the PBS series *House of Cards*. *The Eustace Diamonds,* a novel about Lizzie Holden, a deliciously scheming young woman who marries into an old, rich, aristocratic English family and then attempts to make off with the family jewels, is the closest thing the Victorians had to *Dynasty* and in Lizzie, they had their Alexis.

For all of the melodrama, Trollope himself was a cold and ordered man. He awoke every morning at 5:30 and wrote five pages before going off to his full-time job at the post office, which involved riding around the countryside on a horse, making sure that the mail was being delivered properly. He was contemptuous of anyone who couldn't sit down and knock off exactly five pages in an hour and a half and thought that they shouldn't bother publishing. Lord knows what he thought of Flaubert, whose goal was to write one perfect sentence a day.

We had developed a particular interest in Trollope a couple of years before. New Year's Day had been unseasonably warm and we had decided to celebrate with a hike to Richmond Point. The trail at Richmond Point is unmarked. It used to be public land, part of the Taconic Trail complex, but the surrounding acreage had been bought privately. The new owner did not mind local people hiking across his land as long as they didn't give away the presence of a trail by parking in front of the entrance. As a result, unlike Monument Mountain, which on a day like that would be crawling with people, the trail to Richmond Point would be peaceful and, at worst, sparsely populated.

It's about two miles from the trailhead to the top and it takes about forty-five minutes. We didn't see another soul. We were completely alone in the woods. Brilliant sunshine filtered through the pine trees. We spent almost the entire hike talking about one of Trollope's *Parliamentary Novels, Phineas Finn.*

Phineas, a young, handsome Irishman, had gotten himself elected to Parliament, but had come to London lacking the means to live appropriately for a man in his position. He had left behind the sweet and pretty local girl, Mary Flood Jones, who in kissing her upon his departure and asking for a lock of her hair, had given every expectation of a proposal of marriage. In London, however, he almost immediately fell in love with the politically astute Lady Laura Standish, the daughter of the Earl of Brentford, who, while perhaps being not quite so good to look at, promised to be a boon to Phineas's career. On the day Phineas proposed, however, Lady Laura decided to marry a different member of Parliament, the staggeringly rich but exceedingly dull Mr. Kennedy.

Phineas pined for a day or two, then promptly fell in love with Violet Effingham, who was beautiful, wild, rich, influential and also the avowed love of Lord Chiltern, Lady Laura's brother and Phineas's best friend. Interwoven with Phineas's amorous adventures was a hilarious, dead-on portrayal of the machinations of Parliament.

So, what happened? Who did Phineas marry? How did he stay

in Parliament without any money? Did he stay in Parliament at all? Did he vote his morals or his party? What happened to Mary Flood Jones? And who was this beautiful, savvy, and rich foreign widow, Madame Max Goesler?

We didn't know.

Sitting at the top of Richmond Point, looking out over hill-tops for miles in every direction, we could only speculate. That was because we didn't have the end of the book. It was the fashion, during the nineteenth century, for novels to be written in three parts and the Lenox library had parts one and two, but not part three, something we hadn't realized when we had taken out the first two.

And now, here, in "Books Bruce & Sue Gventer" was a set of Trollopes, nineteen in all that took up almost half a shelf all by themselves. The set had been published in 1904. They were small and worn. Half of the spines were badly sunned, the other half a crisp maroon. The series was undoubtedly incomplete. But there were nineteen, some of which we had not seen anywhere before, not even in a library. And so what if they weren't in great condition? If we wanted great condition, we could buy the *leatherbounds*. We didn't want condition. We wanted *character*. We also wanted Part III of *Phineas Finn*.

We took down the first book of the set and opened to the price on the inside page. Forty dollars.

We looked over at Bruce. He was huddled at the desk, leaning over a newspaper, one of the local weeklies. He appeared to be considering why he had to freeze just because some lunatics wanted to browse in an unheated bookstore in the middle of winter.

"Is this price right? Forty dollars a book for the Trollopes?"

Bruce reluctantly got up. He walked over to us and looked at the price on the page. "No, no," he said. "Forty dollars for the set."

Forty dollars? Nineteen books for forty dollars? That meant that each book cost . . .

"We'll take them."

"Great," Bruce replied, noticeably more cheerful. In addition to getting rid of nineteen books, he was freeing up a lot of shelf space.

(Those piles of books on the floor might yet acquire a home.) "Should I put them in a box?"

A box, too? "Sure. Thanks."

The "box" was a cardboard carton that said WISE POTATO CHIPS, but even that was a deal. It was wood-fire-every-morning time and cardboard makes the best kindling.

So we took the Trollopes home and arranged them on *our* shelves. They looked very nice. They did add character. And—oh, yes—about Phineas Finn. He does get married, of course, to . . .

No, that would be telling.

That winter, we hit almost every used-book store listed in the Berkshire County Yellow Pages. While other families trundled off to Jiminy Peak or Swift River for a day of downhill or cross-country skiing, we went book hunting. Even our daughter, Emily, who was not quite three, got into the spirit of the thing, although it meant we had to buy a couple of children's books at every stop.

Yellow House Books in Great Barrington was Emily's favorite. Yellow House was owned by Bob and Bonnie Benson, who moved to Lenox from California, where they used to sell used books at outdoor flea markets. Bob was an accomplished, almost-professional-caliber jazz pianist and in the back room, amid the literature, history, philosophy, and music sections, was Nat King Cole's personal piano, which Bob and Bonnie had bought at auction for $16,500. On rainy days (perhaps to celebrate being indoors after their flea market days) Bob would sit and play.

While just about every used-book store has a children's section, it tends to be physically indistinguishable from the other parts of the store, just another bookcase, stuffed with books, four or five feet off the ground. It was clear that owners of used-book stores did not expect children to browse in the children's section. Yellow House was different. They had a separate section of the store for children, complete with a miniature bench and rocking chair and a cozy crawl space filled with toys. Except for a couple of shelves where the more expensive volumes were kept, most of the books were at beginning reader eye-level.

In addition to the usual offerings of contemporary books like Sesame Street, Dr. Suess, and the Berenstain Bears, Yellow House carried illustrated copies of all the classics for ten or fifteen dollars and all those little Golden Books for fifty cents. But better than that were the books with fairy tales from other countries or the older books that nobody reads anymore. Emily loves dinosaurs and we found a hardcover of a terrific book called *Archaeopteryx* for three-fifty.

We also hit Librarium in Chatham, New York, just across the border to the north and Rodgers Book Barn in Hillsdale, just across the border to the south. Both were huge old barns that stocked just about every inch of space with used books of every description, most for under ten dollars. There were lots of paperbacks and books without dust jackets and books without covers and books that were torn or dirty, but they had just about everything.

We found a wonderful Photoplay edition of Booth Tarkington's *Plutocrat* for three dollars on the second floor of Rodgers Book Barn. Photoplay editions were popular in the thirties. They were part of promotions for what were at the time upcoming feature films and contained still photographs of scenes from the movie. Although to our knowledge *The Plutocrat* (or *Business and Pleasure,* as it had been retitled for the movies) was never actually released in the theaters, our copy was in very nice condition and had photographs of Will Rogers, wearing a pith helmet, playing Tinker the industrialist and Joel McCrae, in evening dress, as the callow young playwright Laurence Ogle.

Then, one day, we walked into Farshaw's in Great Barrington. Farshaw's (the name seemed vaguely Shakespearean but was actually a holdover from the army-navy store that had occupied the space previously) was on Railroad Street, past the ice-cream store but not all the way to Gatsby's, which sold bras and wicker furniture. Their advertisement read:

FARSHAW'S BOOKSHOP
old, used and antiquarian

> Farshaw's Bookshop is well worth a visit for anyone who
> enjoys searching for good books at fair prices in an amiable
> environment. We do not specialize in any subjects, but
> tend to have books which, for one reason or another, we
> regard as unusually interesting or important.

At the bottom, it said that Farshaw's was owned by Michael and
Helen Selzer.

Farshaw's was narrow and cramped. Each side wall was lined
floor to ceiling with bookshelves and there was a six-foot-high set of
shelves set right in the middle that ran almost the entire length of the
shop. There was a large glass-topped counter just inside the door, immediately to the left, with books and pamphlets on top, next to an
old-fashioned cash register. Just past the counter, there was a genuine antique barber chair with a shiny green leather seat where a customer could settle in to browse through a potential purchase and a
reading lamp just to the side.

We had stopped into Farshaw's briefly once or twice before.
On those occasions, a man had been behind the counter, who we
had assumed was Michael Selzer. He had appeared to be in his early
fifties with a full beard, longish, perpetually tousled hair, and a well-
rounded figure. He hadn't said much, always seeming to be involved
with something, but managed to exude scholarliness all the same.

This time, a pretty dark-haired woman who appeared to be in
her late forties, wearing eye makeup (a rarity in the Berkshires) and
dressed all in black was behind the counter. She smiled when she saw
us. The smile lit up her face. "Good morning," she said. "Is there
anything special you're looking for?"

"Literature?"

She got out from behind the desk and led us over to the shelves
in the center of the room. "Let me show you how we're set up," she

said. "We lease space to other dealers," she said, pointing to the aisle to the left of the center but walking to the right. "This is *our* fiction," she said, gesturing toward the length of the center bookcase. "The first editions are here," pointing out the first section and a half, "and everything else is in alphabetical order going toward the back of the store. You will find fiction in the other dealer's shelves, but every dealer has his own section and you have to look through each one individually because not all of them have literature and the books aren't arranged in any particular order."

We nodded and thanked her and proceeded to browse. She went back to the desk.

The selection at Farshaw's was very good; literature and mystery occupied the entire side of the center divider. We found a nice copy of *The American* by Henry James for $5.00 and *The Brothers Karamazov* for $6.50. We brought our selections to the desk. We hadn't bothered checking out the other dealers.

The woman began to write out an invoice on one of those little pads that waitresses in diners use to take orders. While we were standing there, our eyes happened to fall on a copy of a book that was standing upright on a little stand. *Disraeli, the Jew* it said, by Michael Selzer.

As we glanced at it, the woman behind the desk looked up. "Oh, that's Michael's book," she said. "It's excellent. It's fifteen dollars. Have you met Michael?"

"Kind of. We've been here once or twice before."

"Michael's my husband. We own this store. I'm Helen. It's really a fascinating book," she went on. "Michael discovered boxes of Disraeli's private papers when he was a student at Oxford. He was in the library and there was something way up on top of some cabinet, a box or something, and Michael made the librarian bring it down. He didn't want to but Michael made him. And they turned out to be Disraeli's private papers! Which nobody knew about all this time! There were even a lot of doodles in there, too. Can you imagine? Disraeli's doodles?" Helen chuckled and went on. "And so Michael had access to all of these new, terrific papers and he wrote a letter to the London *Times* and that's how he got to interview Albert Speer."

"Albert Speer?" Helen's speech was kind of like trying to catch a train as it moved without stopping through a station.

"Yes, Michael's first language is German, you know, his parents were born in Germany but left in 1936, so Michael got this job at the London *Times,* so when they needed someone to interview Speer, you know Speer, at the time, was trying to promote himself as the 'good' Nazi and he actually convinced a lot of people, can you believe that?" Helen shook her head. "In any event, the *Times* picked Michael and they sent him to Spandau and he sat and talked to Speer for a long time. Speer was very cold, very superior, never shook Michael's hand, and then, at the end of the interview, he turned to Michael and said, 'How old are you, young man?' When Michael said that he was thirty-five, Speer said, 'When I was your age, I held an important position in my country's government.'

"Michael has had a fascinating life," Helen continued. "He was the youngest correspondent at the Eichmann trial. Can you imagine, sitting there, near this horrible mass murderer? He had a big fight with Hannah Arendt, you know, the woman with the banality of evil theory. Michael had studied the Rorschach tests of hundreds of Nazis and Nazi collaborators and they were just off the charts, each one, and he told her that there was nothing banal about that."

"How did he get to be the youngest correspondent at the Eichmann trial?"

"His parents were medical students in Germany when Hitler came to power. They just barely got out, to Italy, in 1936, I think, under a Polish passport to escape being sent to Dachau. Italy was Fascist, but they still allowed Jews to study medicine and Michael's parents finished their degrees. But obviously they couldn't stay in Italy. They tried to get into England, but England wasn't letting in refugees unless they worked in the colonies first so Michael's parents went to Lahore, which is in Pakistan now but was still part of India then.

"Two weeks after Michael was born, England declared war on

Germany, after Germany invaded Poland. The British decided to put all the German families in India in internment camps and even though Michael's family were Jews they got thrown in with everybody else. So, for six years Michael and his parents and four other Jewish families were penned up in camps with other people who were saying things like, 'Don't worry. Rommel's coming to save us . . . but not you.' "

"What happened after the war?"

"Oh, after the war was great. You know, everyone in India wanted European doctors, so Michael's parents got rich. Michael led this very privileged life in India. He was like a little maharajah. He was tutored by Capuchin monks. When he wanted to learn to drive a car, he used the runway at the airport and his servants would run out every once in a while and say, 'Please, Sahib, the airplane needs to land now.' When he was ready for school, his parents shipped him off to Bedales and then he went to Oxford and got a degree in Oriental languages."

We didn't know quite what to say but it didn't matter because Helen was off and running again.

"Michael's done everything," said Helen, with a wave and a smile. "When he lived in Israel, in his early twenties, he was being groomed for an important position in the government. But Michael is an anti-Zionist, very outspoken, he got along very well with the Arabs, a lot of people hated him, but he was so controversial that his enemies agreed to give up a cabinet post in order to keep him out. He's interviewed everyone from the Dalai Lama to Ben Gurion. He's traded commodities, he's written books . . . here, let me show you a picture." Helen picked up a book called *Deliverance Day: The Last Hours at Dachau* and opened to the back flap of the dust jacket. There was a picture of a dark, intelligent-looking, fabulously handsome man in his early thirties who bore a striking resemblance to the actor Steven Bauer in *Thief of Hearts*.

"Wow," said one of us.

"Of course, this picture was taken a while ago," said Helen.

"How did you meet him?"

Suddenly, Helen turned bright red. "Oh, it was very romantic," she said. She looked down at the waitress pad. "That will be twelve dollars and eight cents."

CHAPTER 4

In March, we went to Chicago for Ruth's birthday. One afternoon, we left Emily with her grandparents and used the opportunity to check out the used-book stores on the North Side and to visit Ruth and Clarence.

From the Yellow Pages, we had a list of four or five stores that looked promising. They were all in the same general area, near where Lincoln Avenue crosses Clark Street, all but one within walking distance of the others.

We started with the one that had had the biggest ad in the Yellow Pages and, coincidentally, was the only one out of walking distance: Powell's. Powell's turned out to be huge and the first used-book store we'd seen in a long time that reminded us of a university bookstore. Here was the place a person would find the advanced chemistry textbook or a paperback of *Crime and Punishment* for a graduate course in Russian literature. What hardcover fiction Powell's had were clearly remainders of recent books that had had too large a printing, like *Whirlwind* by James Clavell or *Outerbridge Reach* by Robert Stone or breakthrough books by writers who are considered literary but nobody reads, like Harold Brodkey or Paul Auster. They also had a ton of the kind of cookbooks that publishers put out every Christmas that are off the shelves by January 2.

At Powell's it was the nonfiction section that was impressive. The delineations in nonfiction were extremely specific. For example, if you were doing a serious academic treatise on France, you would know just where to look at Powell's. They had medieval French history, Louis XIV, French Revolution, nineteenth-century French history, and modern French history.

We were browsing in the twentieth-century European history section. Browsing at Powell's is harder than at other stores because, once again, the bookshelves were floor to ceiling, but in this case the ceilings were about twelve feet high. To see the books on the top shelves you had to get one of those rolling ladders that are attached to tracks on the ceiling and run the length of the store. It was while we were still on the floor that one of us stopped and pointed to a spot about eight feet up.

"Nancy, I want that book!"

"What book?"

"This one." The ladder was already rolling. *"The Political Education of Arnold Brecht: An Autobiography 1884–1970."*

"Who's Arnold Brecht?"

"When I went to the New School in 1973 there was a fragile, extremely old man who used to sit in the lobby near the cafeteria and he was clearly somebody important. People used to come by all the time and ask permission to sit down and talk with him. One day I asked my advisor, 'Who's that guy?' and he looked at me and said, 'That's Arnold Brecht!' as if I had just asked who Winston Churchill was.

"I knew the name from the catalogue. He was a Professor Emeritus in the Political Science department, which happened to be my major. 'Oh, right,' I said. 'Does he still teach?'

" 'Only a seminar,' said my advisor. 'He's almost ninety.'

" 'Any good?' I asked.

" 'He's brilliant. Haven't you read *Political Theory*?' When I said no, my advisor said, 'You can't be educated without it. It's one of the great books of the twentieth century.'

"During the thirties and forties, the New School established the University in Exile as part of its graduate program. It had a lot of great scholars on the faculty who had fled the Nazis, like Hannah Arendt and Erich Hula. I asked if Brecht was one of them.

" 'More than that,' my advisor said. 'Brecht was a high official in the German government from about 1914 on. He was acting state secretary in 1933, when Hitler came to power. At the opening of Parliament, when Hitler came to the podium, Brecht refused to shake his hand and, in no uncertain terms, he told Hitler exactly why—in front of the entire government. His friends had to smuggle him out of the country in the middle of the night, just before he was scheduled to be arrested.

" 'He knew everyone personally . . . the Communists, the Socialists, the Nazis, and Democrats. He first met Hitler in Munich in 1921, when Hitler was a nobody, stuffing envelopes in a dark room at the back of a beer cellar. He knows as much about Weimar Germany and how and why Hitler came to power as any man still alive.' "

The Political Education of Arnold Brecht turned out to be as gripping and easy to read as first-class fiction, while providing a unique and irreplaceable look at one of the most fascinating periods in recent history. It was now 1994 and Arnold Brecht was gone. We realized that, other than in a used-book store like Powell's or in an occasional university library, *The Political Education of Arnold Brecht* had almost certainly ceased to exist as well.

But *we* had it. A treasure. And it cost $12.50.

A couple of bookstores later, we came to Rohe. Rohe was just the opposite of Powell's. It was a small store, the smallest we had yet visited, no more than three hundred square feet. The entire back sidewall was devoted to literature.

Rohe had a terrific selection of late-nineteenth- and early-twentieth-century midwestern writers, Mark Twain, Booth Tarkington, Sinclair Lewis, Edna Ferber, F. Scott Fitzgerald (although no *Gatsby*), copies in good condition, although usually without dust jackets, for five dollars and under.

It was here that we finally found out who George Ade was. He was a humorist, kind of the Garrison Keillor of his day, except that his stories were set in Indiana. Ade enjoyed nationwide acclaim. He was one of the most popular writers around the turn of the century, right up there with Twain and Tarkington, and considered by many at the time to be superior to both. With gentle satire, he captured perfectly the spirit of small-town America.

"The town had two wings of the Protestant faith," he wrote about the little hamlet of Musselwhite in *To Make a Hoosier Holiday*, "but they did not always flap in unison. They were united in the single belief that the Catholic congregation at the other end of town was intent on some dark plan to capture the government and blow up the public school system."

Rohe also had a section devoted to short story collections. We hadn't seen that before. We were browsing casually through the shelves, when a book caught our eye. We had only seen it once before but we recognized it instantly.

It was an old book and looked it, dull olive with faded gold lettering and a black, checkerboard border. And in it was the story by Booth Tarkington.

We had read it on vacation five or six years before at the American Hotel in Sag Harbor. The American Hotel was a small, historic three-story building with eight rooms and a three-star restaurant with a five-star wine list. There was a parlor complete with big, cushy leather club chairs, backgammon and chess sets, old brandy, and a fireplace. During the season, from Memorial Day to Labor Day, rooms went for upward of two hundred dollars and were almost impossible to get. Especially the ones with the private baths.

We had a great room. A bed with a massive old headboard, large bathroom, antique bureaus, a small, stocked bookcase, and a wrought-iron balcony that looked out over Main Street. And all of this for only $125. That was because we went in early April. It is cold in Sag Harbor in April. We were the only people in the hotel.

It wasn't a long vacation, only three days, but it turned out to be memorable in a number of ways. We woke up early and had breakfast in the restaurant, lolling over wonderful coffee, the *New York Times* and the inestimable Edna's sausage scones. Then we bundled up and took long walks on the beach.

The memory of one of those walks is particularly vivid. It was late afternoon. It was overcast, but the sky was an arresting iron gray. The beach was deserted, desolate, and beautiful at the same time.

We were having a fight. A big one. It was the kind of fight that husbands and wives have during which they think seriously about killing one another. We can no longer remember the subject of this fight, but it seemed important at the time. It was right after one of the tirades that punctuated this fight that we discovered that, sometime during the fight, we had dropped the car keys in the sand. It is unclear in whose pocket the keys were residing when they fell. Each of us was quite insistent about giving credit to the other, which helped the fight along immeasurably.

For almost two hours we searched, retracing our steps, seething, each doing our best to ignore the other. We plodded painstakingly up and down the increasingly windy and ever darkening beach, occasionally stopping at random to sift methodically but hopelessly through some sand. A couple of times we gave up and knocked on the doors of the few houses near that section of the beach, but it was April. No one was there. We were alone. There were no telephones.

Just as the prospect of either sleeping on the beach or trudging miles back to the hotel began to loom large, we found the keys. They were sticking up in the sand, not twenty yards from where we had parked the car.

We returned to the hotel. In the car. Our moods had improved but nowhere near commensurate with our good fortune. We weren't really fighting anymore but we weren't speaking either.

We went directly to our room and each of us carefully chose an activity designed to exclude the other. One climbed into the bathtub, the other plucked a book from the bookcase. For some moments after that, the room was coldly still.

Then:

"Ha," said the person with the book.

Splash, went the person in the bath.

"Ha, ha."

Splash, splash.

"Ha, ha, ha, ha."

Splash, splash, splash.

"Ha, h—"

"What's so damn funny?"

"Nothing." Pause. "Ha, ha, ha, ha."

"Would you please stop that?"

"I can't. It's a very funny story." Pause. "Do you want to read it when I'm done?"

Splashless pause. "Okay."

So endeth the fight.

And now, here it was, in this little bookstore in Chicago. We had never remembered the name of the story, or, like the keys, even would have believed we would have found the book. The story was "Mrs. Protheroe," the book was *Short Story Classics (American), Volume 5.* It was published in 1905 and it was three dollars.

"Hello, hello. Wonderful to see you. Wonderful." Clarence extended his hand. He was dressed in a single-breasted, light gray suit, white shirt, blue tie, and lace-up, polished black shoes. "Nancy, you are as pretty as a picture. Larry, you are looking fit as ever, almost as handsome as me. Just kidding, just kidding. But I'm glad you stopped by. I've got some wonderful things to show you."

"Let them come in first, Clarence," said Ruth, kissing us and then ushering us into the living room. She was dressed in a dark blue silk dress with a white pattern scarf and a small, antique gold bracelet.

As always, the apartment was immaculate.

"Larry, Nancy," Clarence said, walking to a large, glass-fronted bookcase on the far wall, "it's a great adventure you've embarked on. Books are a wonderful avocation, wonderful. You know, some people think it is all right to go out and play golf every morning, and I don't want to criticize, but there is no substitute for great books. Books are like having some of the greatest minds in history in your home. For example, I can pick up Shakespeare or Churchill or Dickens anytime I want."

Clarence opened the glass doors and perused the books on the shelves. He reached in and carefully withdrew a beautifully bound volume.

"This, for example, is *The Pickwick Papers* in a first edition. Very beautiful." He opened the book. There was a slip of paper inside the front cover. "I purchased this from Walter Hill, one of the finest book dealers in the world. He lived right here in Chicago."

Clarence removed the piece of paper and showed it to us.

Walter M. Hill. Catalogue #73. Dickens, Charles. *The Posthumous Papers of the Pickwick Club*. Illustrated by R. Seymour, R. W. Buss and H.K. Browne. 2 volumes, 8 vo, full polished calf, gilt tooled and panelled backs, triple gilt filigree borders, inner borders gilt tooled edges by Riviere, London, 1837. $100. A fine copy of the first edition with a very rare title page of the second volume. Only a very few of these title pages were printed for those subscribers who cared to bind their copies in 2 volumes. With some plates in early states and some of the typographical points of the first issue. Extra-illustration by the insertion of 32 plates designed and engraved by Thomas and published in 1837 by Grattan.

"Riviere was one of the finest binders," said Clarence, rereading the paper over our shoulders. "It says one hundred dollars but I don't think I paid that much. I bought quite a few books from Walter Hill and I think he gave me this for sixty dollars. Maybe he'd had it around for a while and wanted to sell it. Or maybe he was just fond of me. You know, his office used to be in the Marshall Field building—he's dead now, of course—the eleventh or twelfth floor, I can't remember, and I used to go every Saturday afternoon after work at the railroad company. One day he said to me: 'Clarence, I do believe you know my stock better than I do.'

"Oh, yes," Clarence rummaged in his desk and came up with an invoice. "Here it is," he said. "Sixty dollars. Here's the bill."

We looked at the invoice. It indeed said "$60." It also said, "December 5, 1938."

"I have a wonderful *Alice in Wonderland* here," Clarence continued, scanning the bookshelves. "It's not a first, it's a second, but it's very handsomely bound. Wonderful book." He took it out, handed it to us, let us look at it for thirty seconds and then, in his excitement to show us everything, took it back and handed us another. "And here's *The Compleat Angler*. That was the first book I ever bought from Walter Hill. And *The Seven Pillars of Wisdom* by T. E. Lawrence. A great man, T. E. Lawrence."

"You've seen Clarence's books before, haven't you?" asked Ruth.

We had, of course, *seen* them before. Up until now, however, we hadn't really *looked*.

"Here's some Churchill . . . ," Clarence continued.

"The rest are in the linen closet," said Ruth, opening the door. It was true. Churchill had two entire shelves. "We can never find room to put them all," Ruth explained. "They're in the bedroom closet, too."

"I'd like to show you this," Clarence went on, pulling out one volume of a set from the bookcase. "This is the Nonesuch Shakespeare. Beautiful. Feel the leather." He handed us the book. "Oh, and here's the bill. I have it right here. I ordered this set from a British dealer by catalogue."

Charles W. Traylen, Guildford, England. Nonesuch Shakespeare, 7 volumes, £340. The works of Shakespeare. The text of the first folio with quarto variance and a selection of modern readings edited by Herbert Farjeon. The Nonesuch Press, NY, Random House, Inc. 1929. This edition consists of 1,050 copies for sale in Great Britain and Ireland and 550 copies for sale in the United

States of America. Bound in London by A.W. Bain. This is #134. February 9, 1982.

"You know," said Clarence, taking back the Shakespeare, "I remember the first rare book I ever bought. It was *Robinson Crusoe*. I got it from Maggs Brothers in London. I was twenty-eight years old and working all alone on this railroad job in Ohio, picking up the rails and selling them. Selling rails was a new thing then in the United States. I had a big job, I had about forty men working under me, farmers mostly, good hardworking men, and I was making expenses and about three hundred fifty dollars a month, which was very good money back then, but I was lonely. I was always lonesome. So when that book came in the mail and I opened it—I can't tell you how I felt. I felt just great. I was in my room at the hotel all alone and I was so excited when I opened that parcel. That I should own a rare book! It wasn't a rare book—I thought it was, but it wasn't, it wasn't a first—but it had famous illustrations and it was printed in 1790—*Robinson Crusoe* was first printed in 1719.

"But it wouldn't have mattered, it meant so much to me . . . I've remembered that feeling all these years."

CHAPTER 5

*W*e had bought so many books in Chicago that we had to pack them in a big box and ship them home with Emily's stuffed gorilla for company.

Five days later, the package arrived. We took it from the UPS man with great anticipation and immediately brought it inside and opened it. It was wonderful unpacking a big box filled with books, even if we had mailed it to ourselves.

Rohe had been very good to us. In addition to the book of short stories, we had purchased *Arrowsmith, Babbitt,* and *Dodsworth* by Sinclair Lewis and *Mary's Neck, Rumbin Galleries, Alice Adams,* and *Young Mrs. Greeley* by Booth Tarkington. Tarkington won two Pulitzer Prizes and Lewis was the first American to win the Nobel Prize in literature but, unlike Hemingway and Scott Fitzgerald, two other midwestern writers of the 1920s whose reputations have grown over time, Lewis is largely unread and Tarkington has all but disappeared. The price tag for all seven had come in at under thirty dollars.

Tarkington and Lewis were an interesting contrast. They both wrote about the same towns in America, the same time period, even the same kinds of people. But when Tarkington wrote about America, he wrote about the country as it wished (and still wishes) to be seen—essentially kind, gentle, and good, whose faults, if they even were faults, sprung from the unfortunate fact that nobody is perfect. And, like his America, Tarkington's humor was wry, homespun, and endearing.

Lewis wrote about America as it loathed and feared (and still loathes and fears) to be seen—greedy, thoughtless, prejudiced, bullying, and cruel. Like *his* America, Lewis's humor was biting, scathing, cynical, and bitter. *Babbitt* was as vicious an indictment of mainstream America as has ever been put on a page.

Ultimately, Tarkington was beloved and Lewis reviled. When Tarkington needed surgery to save his eyesight, the railroad provided him a private car to transport him across the country to see a specialist. When, later in his life, Lewis resided in Williamstown, Massachusetts, home of Williams College, one of the premier small colleges in America, the school would not invite the Nobel Laureate to teach a course.

The package from Chicago began a period of profligate acquisition. We literally haunted every used-book store within a forty-five minute radius of our house and, in a matter of a few months, we had purchased enough books to fill three new floor-to-ceiling bookcases at an average cost of about eight dollars a book.

Quite a few of the books we bought were by writers we wanted in the house. We found Jules Verne, more Tolstoy, Dostoyevsky, Robert Louis Stevenson, Mark Twain, and Henry James, all in decent hardcover editions for under ten dollars. In a major coup, we purchased a thirty-three-volume 1906 set of *The Complete Works of Kipling* for eighty dollars and the entire eleven-volume set of Will and Ariel Durant's *Story of Civilization* for under seventy dollars. William Saroyan, Edna Ferber, and Joseph Conrad all found their way onto our shelves. There wasn't a weekend that went by that we weren't rearranging our bookcases to accommodate new purchases.

But for all the enjoyment of acquiring the works of writers we wanted, it was the books by writers that we didn't know we wanted that was the most fun.

"Thought you moight loike to try this," said David, walking up to us one day at Berkshire Book Company with a book in his hand. It was *The Chequer Board* by Nevil Shute.

"Didn't he write *On the Beach*?" *On the Beach,* a vision of the last days of human civilization in the wake of nuclear war, had been made into a powerful film starring Gregory Peck and Ava Gardner.

"Roight. That's the one he's most known for anywye. But he wrote lots of other things, too."

We turned the book over in our hands. "Okay. How much?"

"No, no," David said. "Just tyke it. I think you'll enjoy it."

The Chequer Board turned out to be a thoroughly enjoyable, Somerset Maughamesque book about, of all things, a ne'er-do-well Englishman just after World War II with a soon-to-be-fatal head wound who spends his last months seeking out three acquaintances from the war. In the hands of a less talented storyteller, *The Chequer Board* might easily have been alternately grim and sappy, but instead it was alternately gentle and powerful, and ultimately uplifting. As soon as we finished it, we went out and bought *On the Beach*.

Sometimes a book got to us by force of repetition, like *Mid-century* by John Dos Passos. These days, Dos Passos is largely ignored, one of those writers whose name is instantly recognizable to a vastly greater number of people than who have actually read any of his work, a category that included both of us.

Dos Passos was one of the most innovative and preeminent of the Jazz Age novelists and a devastating social critic. In the late 1920s and 1930s no one in American literary circles enjoyed a greater reputation, not Hemingway, not Scott Fitzgerald, not Faulkner. In 1938, Jean-Paul Sartre said simply, "I regard Dos Passos as the greatest writer of our time."

The contrasts with Ernest Hemingway, in particular, are striking. They were born three years and ten miles apart. Each volunteered as an ambulance driver during the First World War and each lived as an expatriate in Paris in the years that followed. They were close friends in Paris, seeing each other virtually every day. It was Dos Passos, already well known for stinging indictments of army life in his first two novels, *One Man's Initiation* (1919) and *Three Soldiers* (1921), who first brought *In Our Time* to the attention of the publisher, Horace Liverwright, in 1925. (*Three Soldiers,* written largely from the point of view of a misfit private, caused a huge stir on publication and is eerily reminiscent of *From Here to Eternity*—or the other way around—which caused an equally big stir and made James Jones a celebrity a generation later.)

In the wake of the Spanish Civil War, Dos Passos and Hemingway ceased to speak and the split was mirrored in their literary fortunes. Hemingway became more and more celebrated, winning the Nobel Prize in literature in 1954, and Dos Passos, although he continued to regularly have his work published, drifted into a kind of literary netherworld, still respected for his early work but considered to have lost both his way and his energy.

It was only in 1961, ironically the year that Hemingway blew his brains out, that Dos Passos reclaimed some of his lost prestige with the publication of *Midcentury,* a book that he had worked on for ten years.

For *Midcentury,* Dos Passos resurrected the same narrative techniques as those used in his most famous works, *Manhattan Transfer* and the *U.S.A.* trilogy, which had been written decades earlier. He painted a kaleidoscopic portrait of American life by interweaving the stories of a number of major characters and adding "newsreels," capsules of factual news of the period, biographies of real Americans representative of the times and what he called "Camera Eye," stream-of-consciousness observations. This time, however, his major target was the corruption of the labor movement rather than the corruption of big business.

Midcentury was a huge commercial success, five printings before publication and four months on the *New York Times* best-seller list. As a result, a copy of *Midcentury* graced the shelves of virtually every used bookstore we visited. Finally, curiosity overwhelmed us and we bought one, a first edition for twelve-fifty.

Midcentury was so good that it made us want to rush out and buy everything we could by Dos Passos. But buying a paperback or taking a copy out of the library was cheating. We checked the "D"s every time we went into a used-book store but, other than a couple of minor works, we simply could not find decent editions of Dos Passos's books.

"Have you ever read anything by Josephine Tey?" asked Esther, during another one of our visits.

"No."

"Ooh, she's quite wonderful," said Esther. "A serious British literary figure, Martin Seymour-Smith, who wrote *Who's Who in Twentieth Century Literature,* reviewed a mystery by Anne Perry recently in the *New York Times Book Review* and he wrote that Perry had modeled her work on Josephine Tey, this forgotten mystery writer of the fifties, and it was such a gratuitous, dismissive remark by someone who obviously didn't read mysteries and didn't know Josephine Tey's work and the fact that she is a figure of some influence among British mystery writers that I always wanted to write a letter to the *Times* and say, far from being forgotten, Josephine Tey's books have never been out of print and it was likely that her books were going to be read when those of the reviewer, as well as the reviewer himself, were long forgotten." Esther was quite red in the face. "It just makes me mad," she said, handing us *Three by Tey,* a 650-page book for ten dollars.

Three by Tey consisted of three short mysteries: *Miss Pym Disposes, The Franchise Affair,* and *Brat Farrar.* All three were wonderful, *The Franchise Affair* in particular, which was an updated version of a famous real-life case in Britain. In 1753, a young girl, Elizabeth Canning, accused two women of kidnapping her, beating her, attempting to force her into prostitution and then, when that failed, keeping her prisoner and compelling her to work as a servant. But, while the stories were interesting, it was the style that made Josephine

Tey so much fun. Everything was understated, laced with subtle wit, the absolute antithesis of the hard-boiled novel. In fact, in *The Franchise Affair,* the detective is a middle-aged, stodgy British country lawyer who lives with his spinster aunt and has digestive biscuits every day for tea.

Josephine Tey was born Elizabeth Mackintosh in Scotland in 1897. She never married and in her twenties moved to Loch Ness to care for her invalid father. She actually attained her greatest fame under another pseudonym, Gordon Daviot. Writing as Daviot she became a very successful dramatist, novelist, and historical biographer, whose plays were performed by, among others, John Geilgud. Like Sir Arthur Conan Doyle, she thought little of detective fiction as a genre and wanted to be remembered for more substantial works, in her case, Gordon Daviot's plays.

In this way, we came to know a number of other terrific writers, people like John Hersey, Somerset Maugham, Evelyn Waugh, and William Dean Howells and wonderful books like *All the King's Men, Andersonville, The Wall, Ashenden,* and *The Blackboard Jungle.* It was easy to take a chance on a book for only five or ten dollars.

The only problem—and it was a small problem—was that, although used-book stores turn over their stock with remarkable frequency, that still did not mean that you could go to the same three or four places week after week and continually find new stuff.

CHAPTER 6

*S*o, when birthday time rolled around the next year, there was no competition. We actually agreed on what we wanted to do—leave Emily overnight with the baby-sitter (a first), stay at an elegant hotel, eat pasta at one of those intimate little restaurants in the North End, and wander through historic Boston, checking out the used-book stores.

Negotiations began at once with the baby-sitter, Claire. We had originally hired Claire on the basis of extraordinary references from extremely reputable people. It was good that she had those references because the rest of her résumé was somewhat nontraditional.

Claire was seventy-two years old and a great-grandmother. She cut and stacked her own wood, drove an ancient pickup truck, was very active during hunting season, had an enormous, extremely unfriendly German shepherd, and wore false teeth. When she came over, invariably dressed in her two-piece bubble-gum pink sweat suit, she would sometimes bring us pirated videotapes of her favorite movies, such as *Dying Young* and *Sleeping with the Enemy*.

At one point, Claire took in a mentally disabled World War II veteran as a border because the Department of Social Services paid her seven hundred dollars a month to "provide him with a noninstitutional environment." The veteran (we never learned his name), apparently did little more than sit around the house, watch television, eat whatever Claire fed him, and go to sleep. He was amiable enough but almost never spoke. When he died a few months later (the cause being unclear), Claire noted sentimentally, "Good riddance to the bastard. I'll miss the money, though."

Of course, we weren't blind to these eccentricities, but there were two factors in our continuing to employ Claire. First, she was, as the references had insisted, remarkable with small children and utterly trustworthy when it came to their care. Emily adored her. Secondly, she was absolutely always available, other residents of Lenox possibly not holding the same ecumenical view of her as ourselves.

"How much do you want to stay overnight?" we asked Claire, the next time we saw her.

We had had a long discussion about this. For obvious reasons, we wanted to err on the side of generosity. We assumed that she would ask for fifty or sixty dollars, to which we would gallantly reply: "Take seventy-five."

Without blinking, Claire replied: "What about a hundred fifty?"

"A hundred fifty dollars?" we repeated. "For one night?"

"Well, you asked me," she returned righteously.

The baby-sitting question thus deftly handled, we went to the Lenox library and photocopied the "Book Dealers—Used & Rare" page of the Boston Yellow Pages. There were thirty listings. We didn't want to waste our time so we took the photocopy to David and Esther to ask their advice on who to visit.

"This one is good," David said, pointing to a listing for a shop in a northwest suburb. "Quoite an extensive selection." He also recommended a couple of stores in Cambridge. With one or two exceptions, he had dismissed most of the listings in Boston proper. "Very proicy," he noted.

So, at about ten o'clock on a late August morning, already $150 in the hole, armed with our photocopy, a street map of the city and its environs, and two terrific head colds, we set off on the two-hour drive to Boston.

We had carefully plotted our route and the shop that David had recommended in the northwest suburb was the strategic first stop, then down through Cambridge and on to our hotel.

The suburb in question consisted of frame houses, pizza parlors, doughnut shops, Laundromats, and beauty parlors. We spotted the bookstore on a corner, pulled into a parking spot, put our two quarters in the meter ($150.50), and went in.

David was right. There certainly were a lot of books. Maybe thirty or forty thousand in all. Unfortunately, there was only space for about ten thousand. Management had solved this problem by building the shelves impossibly close together (even by used-book store standards) and doubling up the books on each shelf. To know what was really on a shelf you had to pull out all the books in the front row in order to see the titles in the back.

On top of that, it was so dark and dusty that someone standing at the other end of the room appeared to be floating in a haze. But we'd just driven two hours to get here, it was our romantic birthday celebration, and, damn it, we were going to 'ave fun.

Moreover, we didn't want to prejudge anything. We were, after all, relative newcomers and it wouldn't do to be dismissive. Also, although this was not our idea of an inviting place to browse, it apparently was other people's. There were five or six other customers in the store. They were dressed uniformly in flannel shirts (it was ninety-two degrees outside), army-navy store jackets, and had a lot of hair, none of it combed. Each of them was puttering about, browsing in utter contentment, slowly and methodically working their way down a shelf inch by inch, looking through every single book the store had in that section. They looked like they had been at it for some time—days maybe. We got the feeling that our fellow patrons spent a good deal of their time indoors.

We started in the literature section. Although in theory, everything was laid out alphabetically, as in "Books Bruce & Sue Gventer," the filing system was casual. Not only were "S"s often found under "G," but hardcovers and paperbacks were intermixed. Many of the books were in appalling condition, sometimes missing front covers or, worse, entire pages. Still, trying to get into the spirit of the thing, we pored around and even got down on our hands and knees (no mean feat in that place) and, for five or ten minutes, pulled out one book after another to see if some treasure would be exposed in the back row. Not only was this search unfruitful, it kicked up a lot of extra dust that resulted in a good deal of sneezing.

"We've got to get out of here," one of us finally rasped to the other, "I can't breathe."

"No. We're here already. Let's at least try to find one book."

So, wiping our noses, we trudged up to the front desk. There was a woman sitting there who looked a perfect match for the patrons. "Do you have *The Guns of August* in hardcover?" we asked.

She thought for a moment. "Well, did you check History?" she said, but before we could answer she continued: "But it might be in War or maybe Political Science." She popped out from behind the desk. "All of those are downstairs. Come on, I'll show you."

We started to say "No, thanks, that's all right," but she was already around the corner leading us, so we followed.

She went to a tiny, narrow space between two shelves that housed a staircase. The staircase was so steep that it was little more than a glorified ladder. "Watch your head," she cautioned.

Two steps down, there was a concrete ledge that we had to bend forty-five degrees to get past. Across it was labeled WATCH YOUR HEAD.

Downstairs turned out to be the basement. This was an old building. Lots of pipes.

"Watch your head," the woman said again.

The shelves were packed so close together and the aisles were so narrow that when the woman walked ten feet and took a left turn, she completely disappeared. We walked around trying to find her and got completely lost.

"Where are you?"

"Over here!" the woman's voice rebounded.

We found her. She was standing in a corner surrounded by shelves. "History is here," she said, pointing. "War is two aisles down and Political Science is in the other corner."

Then, making no effort to see if *The Guns of August* was there, she took two steps, made a right turn, and disappeared again.

After a cursory glance over the shelves, it occurred to us that our time would be better spent trying to find our way out of the basement than looking through all those shelves (doubled, of course) for the Tuchman. We climbed back up the ladder.

"Couldn't find it?" the woman said. "Come back another day. We're always getting new stock."

We slunk out of the store, got a soda at the first doughnut shop we came to, and broke into a package of Tylenol cold capsules.

We decided to skip Cambridge, go straight to the hotel, have lunch, and start over. We were staying at the Copley Plaza. In the spirit of the trip, we had chosen an older hotel, elegantly appointed, which prided itself on beautiful rooms and exemplary service.

We drove up to the Copley, then waited a few minutes outside while the valet parker unloaded a Mercedes that had pulled in behind us and ushered its occupants inside. When he returned, we left our car and walked unescorted to the front desk, our bags, we were assured, to follow.

"Reservation for Goldstone, please."

The desk clerk checked the computer. "Ah, yes. A double room for one night at our special weekend rate." He took out a little rate card and, using an unopened ballpoint pen to point, continued, "The room will be two hundred twenty dollars plus city, state, and hotel occupancy tax."

"Does that include parking?"

"No. I'm afraid not."

"Breakfast?"

"No."

"A newspaper?"

"You may purchase a newspaper in the lobby," he answered coldly.

We must have gotten a special weekend room as well. During the week, it was probably a closet. If we opened the door to the television cabinet/chest of drawers, it blocked our way to the bathroom. There was a place, however, to plug in a portable computer or a fax machine. We debated as to whether or not to call Claire and check if everything was all right, but when we noticed that there was a two-dollar service charge to access an 800 number, we decided to be judicious with our telephone calls.

All right, we decided. So what? We had not come to Boston to hang around our hotel room. We freshened up (use of the bathroom was free), stowed our trusty Yellow Pages photocopy in a backpack, and went to have lunch.

One thing we missed in the Berkshires was the civilized lunch. Not that there isn't good food in the Berkshires; it's simply that lunch is considered a much more casual affair, jeans and sneakers in the summer, jeans and snow boots the other nine months of the year. As a result, we craved fashion as much as food. We ached to people-watch. So, a few days before we left, we had looked through the Zagat's guide, which was available on our computer service and, based upon the following review, booked a reservation at Mamma Maria in the North End:

> "Intimate" and "romantic," this North End "upscale Italian" with "superb little rooms" is "expensive but nice for a special occasion."

Zagat's was right. Mamma Maria's had white tablecloths and fresh roses on the tables. There was an attentive waiter in a black jacket with a towel over his arm. We walked in and were ushered immediately to the best table in the house. Of course, except for the staff, we were the only people *in* the house. We checked our watches. It *was* lunchtime.

"Where is everybody?" we asked the waiter.

"It's August. Vacations," he explained, handing us the menus with a flourish.

We examined our menus and conversed in hushed tones. It felt a little odd to be the only people there. It was kind of like when the gangster forces the restaurant to open out of season so he can impress his moll.

We put down our menus. The waiter was there before they hit the tablecloth.

We ordered seafood salad and pasta. We had originally intended to order wine, but refrained. The cold capsules were beginning to kick in.

The food arrived.

"How's . . . (sniff) . . . yours?"

"Delicious . . . (sniff) . . . and yours?"

"Wonderful."

In truth, neither of us could taste a thing. The food *seemed* great, though.

Lunch (without wine) came to sixty dollars. We were closing in on five hundred dollars and we hadn't bought a single book yet.

For reasons that we cannot for the life of us remember, we decided to walk back to the Copley Plaza from the North End. The humidity was at a level generally found in, say, Costa Rica and our clothes became completely stuck to us before we had gone six steps from the restaurant. We had to run across the plaza where the major thoroughfares that divide the North End from the rest of the city intersect, inhaling visible particles of soot that hung in the air in carcinogenic suspension.

The only bookstore we would pass was Brattle, conveniently located halfway along our route. Brattle advertised itself as a used-book store with a large stock. It was, according to the ad in the Yellow Pages, "Boston's oldest book store." It had also been one of David's choices, although David's opinion was not held in quite as high esteem as it had been when we had left earlier that morning. Nonetheless, after the highways, we looked on Brattle the way the parched legionnaire looks on the oasis.

"Think it's air-conditioned?"

"Sure. It must be."

We found Brattle on a little side street off the Common, down from a fast-food pizza place and right next door to a reading room for lawyers. It was three stories high, stuffed with books, and very definitely not air conditioned.

"Should we stay? It's stifling in here."

"It's worse outside."

"Are you sure?"

Actually, we saw immediately that Brattle was going to be worth a little discomfort. There was an enormous selection, the books were generally in good condition, and there was no intermingling of hardcovers and paperbacks. While Brattle also doubled its shelves, at least the back row was raised so you could get some idea of what you were looking at without having to pull out the books in the front.

We scored almost immediately. In the back row of the Vietnam section we found one of the books we had been looking for, *The Best and the Brightest* by David Halberstam, the Pulitzer Prize–winning study of the men in the Kennedy administration who drew the country into Vietnam. We pulled it out and looked at the front endpaper. Ten dollars. What a deal.

Then we remembered to check. Sure enough. No price on the dust jacket and the telltale stamp on the lower right-hand side of the back cover. A book club edition.

Still, in a year of looking, we had never seen *The Best and the Brightest* before and, book club or no, the copy was in good condition. We decided to buy it. For ten dollars, we reasoned, we could always replace it if we found a better one.

We were browsing around on the second floor when we saw another staircase with a little sign next to it. RARE BOOKS AND FIRST EDITIONS, THIRD FLOOR it said, with a little arrow pointing up.

At this point, beyond the little we had seen and heard from Clarence, we lacked a real sense of what a "rare book" was and what we saw on Brattle's third floor was disappointing. The rare books were not in glass cases as they had been in Clarence's apartment; they were in the same knocked-together pine-board bookcases as the five-and-ten-dollar used books downstairs. And they certainly weren't beautiful and well cared for, like Clarence's *Pickwick Papers* or *Alice in Wonderland*. They were old and beat-up looking, many with yellowed or brown-spotted pages, and some of the spines were so damaged that you couldn't read the titles. They were grouped by subject, pretty much mimicking the rest of the store, except that up here, most of the titles referred to esoteric subjects like the history of small towns in Massachusetts.

In the back section on the left were sets, many of which seemed neither old nor especially rare. There was a six-volume set of Sandburg's *Lincoln,* for example, published in the 1950s that, while nice-looking although not exceptional, was selling for $175. That seemed like a lot of money for a set that we were sure was readily available elsewhere. There was a set of the complete works of Charles Dickens, bound in green leather, not in especially good shape, for $450.

Opposite the sets was a freestanding bookcase that said FIRST EDITIONS. While we obviously had deduced that a first edition was the first printing run of a particular book, here also, we lacked any real sense of why this should be important. We knew people collected first editions, of course, and that they often sold for a lot more money than other editions, but it seemed silly to us to pay a lot of money for a book for no other reason than what amounted to an accident of birth.

We had, for example, bought the fourth printing of *To Kill a Mockingbird* for ten dollars. It looked—and read—exactly the same as the first edition. The only difference that we could see (besides the price) was that our copy read "Fourth Printing" on the copyright page instead of "First Printing." Since we had decided to build our library based on what was *in* the books, it seemed foolish to us to waste our money. Of course, we had been as yet unable to find any editions of books we wanted like *The Great Gatsby, Dracula,* or *Mrs. Bridge,* but we assumed that this was just a matter of time and patience.

Nonetheless, it was always interesting to look. The first-edition section was rather small by Brattle standards, only two or three sections of a six-foot-high bookcase. For our taste, it was not a particularly impressive selection. Nothing we wanted was there. Many of the books looked like they could have been had in a new-book store. There were a lot of Robert B. Parkers.

We were just about to leave when we saw B. Traven's *Night Visitor and Other Stories.*

The Night Visitor had haunted us, almost literally, for five years. Before we were willing to abandon the city and move to the Berkshires, as a final test of our commitment, we had decided to spend a winter there. Not having a good deal of money to spend (or any money to spend, for that matter) we had followed a friend's suggestion and put an ad in the local newspaper, offering ourselves up as house sitters.

We received a response from a couple who owned a huge, dark, drafty old farmhouse that they had inherited from a great-uncle, whom they referred to as "Ainge." It turned out that Ainge had been a member of the Communist Party and an operative of the leftist underground. (During the course of our stay, we discovered that the house had a secret bedroom that you could access only from a trapdoor in one of the back bathrooms and that had served as a hideout for other Communists on the run in the 1930s. Snooping around further, we also discovered that "Ainge" was short for "Friedrich Engels.")

The current owners, Dan and Katherine, offered what seemed to us to be extremely reasonable terms. We could stay rent-free, paying only for the heating oil and electricity. We jumped at the chance to spend the winter in such a romantic setting and, congratulating ourselves on our coup, wondered why the owners did not take advantage of it themselves.

It didn't take us long to figure out why Dan and Katherine did not spend their winters in Uncle Ainge's house. It was freezing. Even with every door and window in the place closed, you could still feel the wind whistling its icy way through the living room, around the study, up the stairs, and into the bath. The house contained only one thermostat, which was located about five feet from the fireplace, so that if you chose to make a fire and stem the hemorrhaging of fuel oil, you couldn't walk anywhere else in the house without seeing your breath. It would have been unnecessary to put food into the refrigerator in that house, except for the mice. There were a lot of mice. There seemed to be a lot of other things, too, judging from the constant sounds of chewing in the basement and the attic.

It turned out to be an authentic New England house in an authentic New England winter. Modern conveniences were scarce. The oven didn't work and you had to risk personal immolation lighting the burners on top of the stove. We had to go into town to wash our clothes, although Dan and Katherine did have a working dryer (we were often tempted to sleep in it). There was no cable service and, because the house was in a valley, reception on radio and television was limited to one fuzzy station each.

But one thing Uncle Ainge's house had was books.

Uncle Ainge had apparently been one of your more intellectual Communists. There were bookshelves everywhere, stocked with a fabulous (and, as we now realize, immensely valuable) collection of books, pamphlets, magazines, correspondence, and records, mostly the writings of old socialists. A good deal of the material was academic but there was also no shortage of literature. People like Jack London, Upton Sinclair, John Dos Passos, and hundreds of others that we had never heard of. Each night, we took a volume from the shelves, got into our long johns, piled on every blanket that we could find, got into bed early, and read by the forty-watt light of the little lamps on the bedside tables. Books that one reads under these circumstances tend to be rather memorable.

One of the books we read that winter was *The Night Visitor and Other Stories* by B. Traven.

"The Night Visitor" is a ghost story written by a ghost. B. Traven himself did not exist. The search for the true identity of the man who wrote under that name is one of the great mysteries of literature. It has obsessed hundreds of people over the years, spawned numerous theories and articles, and was the subject of a documentary on the BBC. The copy on the dust jackets of his books each sport a different biography, depending on which theory was in vogue at the time of publication. Despite immense research, Traven's origins continue to remain indistinct. The early prevalent belief that he was either Traven Torsvan or Hal Croves, born in either Minnesota or Chicago, has evolved. A strong case can now be made that he was either the illegitimate son of Kaiser Wilhelm the Second of Germany or the son of a bricklayer, born in a small town in Poland. It has been established with some certainty that, at one point, whoever he was before, he became Ret Marut, an actor and radical leftist who published forbidden revolutionary pamphlets in Bavaria in the closing days of World War I and escaped a death sentence in Germany only hours before he was to be arrested. He left the country as a seaman on a tramp freighter, an experience he described in his first book, *The Death Ship,* published after he landed in Mexico sometime in 1919. He subsequently migrated to Chiapas, Mexico's southernmost province, where he continued his hazy existence, living in the jungle and becoming a hero to the local Indian population while sending his work off to Germany to be published. Although his major achievement was a six-book series detailing the events that led up to the Mexican Revolution, he is best known to Americans as the author of *The Treasure of the Sierra Madre,* a book which few people have actually read, although almost everyone has seen the film.

The Night Visitor is a riveting collection of stories, each set in the jungles of Chiapas. They are a combination of Edgar Allan Poe and Ernest Hemingway (to whom Traven has often been compared), only better.

We had wanted this book ever since. And here it was. But it was a first edition. The price was forty-five dollars.

We almost put it back. Even though we knew that there was a distinct possibility that we would not see this book again for years, even though we both desperately wanted it, we almost put it back.

We had been perfectly willing (if not completely thrilled) to spend two hundred plus on a hotel, a hundred and fifty on a homicidal septuagenarian baby-sitter, and sixty dollars on a lunch we couldn't taste. These were acceptable expenses. This was simply what these things cost if we wished to partake of them. But forty-five dollars for an old book, not even a particularly large book, was *an extravagance*. It was *wasteful*. What would we tell our parents?

"We can't do this. We're not going to start buying first editions."

"Oh, don't be ridiculous. Of course we're not going to start buying first editions. This is just one book. Do you want it or not?"

"Of course I want it."

"Then let's buy it. Call it a birthday present."

"We should wait and see if we can find it in another edition."

"There *aren't* any other editions."

"Well, all right. But I'm telling you, we're not going to start spending forty-five dollars on first editions."

"Fine."

We bought the book.

The second we walked out of Brattle we knew we had made the right decision. When we got home we put that book on our shelves and for months afterward not a day went by when we didn't look at it.

And, to this day, whenever we pass by the shelf and look at *The Night Visitor,* we again see that old farmhouse, complete with mousetraps, again feel the way we'd felt when we'd first read the stories, and realize it *had* been a romantic winter after all.

CHAPTER 7

*P*urchasing *The Night Visitor* gave us so much pleasure, and we were so pleased and proud to have it, that we realized that up until that point we had been narrow-minded. *Of course* it was all right to buy a first edition of a book that was important to us. In fact, we *should* have first editions of books that were important to us. *Important* was the key word here. We certainly had no intention of running out and gobbling up every forty-five-dollar book we saw. Why, it might be another year before we found a volume important enough to merit addition to our first-edition section.

About two weeks later, we went to Farshaw's. This time, Michael was behind the desk.

"Good afternoon," he said. Michael had a rich, not especially deep voice and spoke with an accent that was at once perfectly British and vaguely German. "Is there anything in particular that you are looking for?"

We said hello, that we just wanted to look, and walked past him to browse through the store. As before, we headed to the literature section on the right side of the center aisle. We found *The Witches of Eastwick* and a nice copy of *The Chosen* for $8.95.

(*The Chosen* had always had a special meaning for Larry's family. Years before, when Larry was in high school, his family had lived in Brooklyn, on East Eighth Street. A rabbi named Chaim Potok moved into the apartment downstairs. Whenever Larry's parents came home late at night, a light was always on in the rabbi's apartment. "Maybe he's writing a book," his mother joked.)

When we had finished, instead of just going to the desk and paying, we went around to the sections that Michael and Helen rented to other dealers. In a section labeled STEPHEN AND KATHLEEN LUPACK, MERIDAN, CT, on the third shelf down, was *Nineteen Eighty-four*.

We took the book off the shelf and opened the cover. "1st US," it read. "$100."

We looked it over. It seemed to be in excellent condition.

"Don't we have this?"

"I don't think so. Maybe in paperback."

"Maybe." We were fondling the book now. "Too bad. This is a great book. You've read it, haven't you?"

"In high school."

"You should read it again. You can't appreciate it in high school."

"It's a hundred dollars."

"I know. We can't buy a hundred-dollar book. It's out of the question. Let's just put it back."

"Right." The book had not left our hands.

"Too bad. It's a great book. It's probably a good deal. Orwell certainly won't drop in value."

"No, Orwell won't."

"That's the good thing about firsts. You know they won't drop in value."

"That's true." As if we had any idea at all of what we were talking about.

"That means if we wait it will only go up in value."

"So we're probably actually saving money if we buy it now."

"Look, we just can't spend a hundred dollars on a book."

"Right."

When we took our purchases to the desk, Michael was embroiled in a spirited political discussion on an indeterminate topic with an intense, unshaven man of about thirty. Michael began absent-mindedly opening the covers, glancing away from the unshaven man to look at the prices and write them down on the waitress pad . . . $8.95, $5.00, $6.50. Then he came to *Nineteen Eighty-four.*

He stopped and looked up. "What exactly do you collect?" he asked.

Up until that moment, we had never felt like we "collected" anything. We were just two people who bought used books.

"Uh, we only buy books we like to read."

"How unusual." Michael paused. "Have you ever seen any of *our* books?"

Without waiting for an answer, he led us to a locked glass cabinet on the wall on the left-hand side of the shop. Inside the cabinet was a little sign that read SELZER & SELZER ANTIQUARIAN BOOKS. With a small flourish, he unlocked the cabinet.

"Here is something that you might find interesting," he said, reaching in to withdraw a book with a faded green-and-yellow dust jacket. It did not appear any different—and certainly no more valuable—than any other of the hundreds of five- and-ten-dollar books on the open shelves. It was a copy of Gabriel García Márquez's *One Hundred Years of Solitude.*

"This book has an unique history," he said, placing it into our hands. We were surprised that he let us hold it.

"It's a first, of course," Michael continued. "It was originally published in Argentina in 1967 as *Cien años de soledad.* Harper and Row bought the rights and published this American edition in 1970. It sold quite poorly, and, after a while Harper and Row had the remainders pulped, little suspecting, of course, that Márquez would go on to win the Nobel Prize." He chuckled. "That left the few thousand copies that had sold as the only survivors of the first printing. We are asking four hundred dollars for this one, which is a really re-markable price."

While that did indeed turn out to be a remarkable price (we have since seen *One Hundred Years of Solitude* sell for upward of $750), $400 was still substantially too remarkable for us. We looked at each other, then at the book, turning it over and riffling through the pages as if we were actually considering buying it.

"Uh, it's a very good book," we floundered, "but not exactly wh . . ."

Michael nodded and relieved us of the Márquez. The second it left our hands, we wanted it back.

Michael replaced *One Hundred Years of Solitude* and withdrew another, a small, reddish decrepit volume with no dust jacket. There were no identifying markings on either the cover or the spine. We stared at it, trying to figure out what it was. By now we understood that there would be a story here, something special about this book.

The idea that books had stories associated with them that had nothing to do with the stories inside them was new to us. We had always valued the history, the world of ideas contained between the covers of a book or, as in the case of *The Night Visitor,* some special personal significance. Now, for the first time, we began to appreciate that there was a history and a world of ideas embodied by the books themselves.

"We picked this item up at an auction," Michael began. "It has wonderful historical relevance." He paused. He was very good at pauses. "This may be the first American edition of one of the great works of the twentieth century," he went on. "Unofficial as it may be."

We took the volume, holding it gingerly. We were not sure that if it disintegrated in our hands, we would not be required to pay for it.

"You will notice the square shape," he continued. We did no-tice. "If you open it, you will also notice the absence of a title page or any other indication of what may lay inside."

He paused again. We were forced to risk actually opening the book and peeking under the cover.

"It is *Ulysses,*" he announced with a flourish somewhat larger than his flourish when he unlocked the glass case. "It was, as you know, banned in this country. This copy was intentionally printed in square format and bound without markings so that, if an unlettered customs agent stumbled across it, he would be unaware that he was holding a piece of contraband that was being smuggled into the country."

It was a fascinating story. We were sure that another remarkable price was in the offing.

"Being that this is not a true first edition, we have priced this copy at four hundred fifty dollars, which, considering the significance, is very fair."

We assured Michael that his price was more than fair. Nonetheless, that didn't mean we could afford it.

Michael returned *Ulysses* to the cabinet. We wistfully watched it go. He removed a sheaf of old papers. "Perhaps this remarkable pamphlet . . ."

"Going to the book fair?" asked David.

It was about a month after that, in early October. We had just finished writing him a check for $128, ninety of which was for a first edition of *East of Eden* by John Steinbeck, a book that neither of us had read but we had both seen the movie. Obviously, even in that thirty days, the concept of "important" had been substantially diluted.

A number of other first editions had found their way to our shelves as well. At Second Life Books, which is located on the side of a mountain in Lanesborough on a road not for the faint of heart and for which it is advisable to have four-wheel drive, and where, not surprisingly, most of the business is done by mail order, we had found first American editions of two other novels by B. Traven, *The Rebellion of the Hanged* and *The General from the Jungle* at the bargain price of thirty-five dollars each. (We had virtuously albeit reluctantly passed up a first American edition of *The Death Ship* for $250.) At other shops, we had also purchased firsts of Norman Mailer's *Armies of the Night* and *The Right Stuff* by Tom Wolfe for what seemed like the ridiculously low price of fifteen and ten dollars, respectively. We had been unable for the life of us to figure out how these prices were set but that had not prevented us from paying them.

"Book fair? What book fair?"

"The one in Sheffield, at the hoigh school, on Satahday."

"Would we like it?"

"Oh, yes. It's quoite noice. You should definitely try it. There'll be a lot of dealahs with quoite a number of excellent books. And it's not as expensive as the big fairs, loike New York or Boston."

"Are you going?"

He paused. "I usually send Esthah."

We had been to fairs before, of course, mostly street fairs in New York or school and garden fairs in the Berkshires. We expected much the same thing from a book fair—lots of food interspersed with stalls or stands manned by bored-looking artisans who only perk up if you look like you might buy something.

The first thing we noticed that was different about a book fair was that we had to pay to get in. This one was three dollars a ticket although, after we had slapped down our six bucks, we saw a lot of little blue cards that said, "Sheffield Antiquarian Book Fair. One dollar off admission price with this ticket. Sponsored by Books Bruce & Sue Gventer."

The event was being held at Mount Everett Regional High School, a spanking new building built amid much controversy and even more expense. We handed in our tickets and walked into the gym where most of the dealers had set up. There were rows and rows of stalls that, due to the space limitations, were packed a good deal closer together than at outdoor fairs. The presence of the ceiling and artificial light gave the place a closed-in, bazaarlike quality, and, between that and the crowd, the effect was not unlike some exotic, far-flung outpost of the British Empire in the 1930s, replete with a swarm of ragtag refugees waiting for exit visas aimlessly milling about under the keen observation of informers, double agents, and agents provocateurs lurking in the corners. At any moment, we expected to find Peter Lorre tugging at our elbows offering us Letters of Transit.

Here, men and women with little stick-on name tags were constantly shuttling between booths, surreptitiously whispering and passing books and money to each other. As soon as someone without a name tag approached, both conversation and commerce stopped. The customers, for their part, were slinking stealthily across the floor, taking books off the shelves and, with little jerky motions, snapping open the front cover, snapping open the back cover, checking under the dust jacket, then snapping the book back into place before silently moving on.

It was the first time we had ever gone to a place where the people around us were bona fide book collectors (or so we assumed). One of the first things we noticed was the amazing variety of subject matter. There were dealers who specialized in the history of New England, guns, war (there was a lot of war), Churchill, birds (there were even more birds), crafts, and an extraordinary number of cookbooks. There were books that we could not understand why anyone would want to read. There were law reports from the 1850s, old medical books, texts on accounting from the 1920s, minutes of town meetings and ladies' societies. There were lithographs of flowers and insects, maps of towns in northern Maine, and cracked photographs of obscure Civil War generals. There were a number of dealers specializing in children's books—Dr. Seuss, the Hardy Boys, Nancy Drew, the Bobbsey Twins—but, as far as we could see, not a single actual child was in the place. But then again, not too many five year olds have fifty dollars to slap down for a first edition of *Angelina Ballerina*.

And then there were the books we *did* want to read.

"Look at this!"

"What is it? Let me see."

"It's *The Thin Man*."

"Wow! Neat! Look at that great dust jacket. How much?"

We opened the cover to the front endpaper. Pencilled very delicately were the words "1st. $2,500."

We looked up. The dealer, a sallow, underweight, middle-aged man wearing a short-sleeved checked shirt, was looking at us, sizing us up, trying to decide if we were real buyers. Even though he looked like he could barely afford Kraft macaroni and cheese for dinner, *he* was the one with the twenty-five-hundred-dollar book.

"Uh, very nice," we said and put it back so quickly we almost dropped it.

We saw a first U.K. *and* a first American edition of Sherlock Holmes. We saw Raymond Chandler, H. G. Wells, and Graham Greene all in first edition. There was Kipling, Le Carré, James Jones, and James Joyce; Hemingway, Steinbeck (everywhere), and Truman Capote. We got used to opening up a book and seeing one or two digits with a lot of little penciled zeroes after them on the inside covers. If this was the low price fair, "not loike New York or Boston," what were *they* loike?

For the first time, we saw the sort of fiction that people collected, and we wanted it. Within five minutes, we knew that there was not the slightest possibility of our walking out of that book fair without buying *something*. In that instant we became the kind of people about whom salesmen at used car lots dream.

We had been browsing for about an hour when we came to a stand against the far wall. It was one of the smaller stands, just three chin-high bookcases pushed together to form a U. Three middle-aged men, all wearing short-sleeved button-down shirts with the little name tag stickers on their pockets, were standing close by, talking conspiratorially. It was hard to hear what they were saying but it seemed to be on the order of dealers who had either bought something at a ridiculously low price or sold something at a ridiculously high one. None of the three paid the slightest attention to us.

We started examining the books on the shelves. There were a lot of books we liked, many we hadn't seen before. We took out *The Moon Is Down* by John Steinbeck and opened the cover. "1st edition," it said. "$175." We were immediately pleased. *Our* Steinbeck had only been ninety dollars. So what if it was a different book?

We put back *The Moon Is Down* and took down *The Remains of the Day* by Kazuo Ishiguro. This was when the movie was still going strong. "1st UK edition," it said. "$350."

We put it back. We took down *The Berlin Stories* by Christopher Isherwood and opened it. "1st edition—1945," it said, in a little pencil scrawl. "A beautiful bright copy, uncommon in this condition, $95."

We examined the book closely. It was in excellent condition.

"We have this in paperback, but these stories are terrific," one of us commented to the other.

Immediately, one of the three men standing nearby tore himself away from his conversation with the other two dealers and quickly sidled over.

"May I help you with something?" he said.

"Uh, well, we were just looking—"

"What do you collect?"

There was that question again. "Uh . . ."

"Are you interested in modern firsts?" he continued.

That sounded good. "Yes," we said.

"That's a very good copy," he said, nodding toward the book in our hands. "You don't often see that book in such good condition."

"No," we agreed.

"All the books on these shelves came from Terry Southern's library, you know," he said, indicating the row that Isherwood had come from. "There's no bookplate, but I have the entire collection on consignment. He was an important collector."

"Really." He could have said it was from John F. Kennedy's library and we wouldn't have known the difference. All the same, the book started to look even better.

"*The Berlin Stories* is where they got *Cabaret* from, you know," he added. "The only reason I'm selling this for so little is that I was asked to dispose of the library as quickly as possible."

We looked again at the shelves. All the books seemed to shine in their little plastic covers. We looked at those shelves and thought: that's how we want our bookcase to look.

Still, ninety-five dollars. Our asset base was not sufficiently strong that we could continue to plop down ninety and one hundred dollars for books. We didn't want to find ourselves breaking into our daughter's piggy bank to pay for Ernest Hemingway.

Also, was this what we really wanted? Perhaps there was something else that would be even better. He had Faulkner. We wanted the Snopes trilogy; maybe we could start with *The Hamlet.*

For some reason, he didn't have *The Hamlet,* but he did have *The Town,* which was the second book of the three. We reached up and got that one. It, too, was in superb condition. "1st edition," it said inside. "$60."

Well, all right, that wasn't so bad. We could always pick up *The Hamlet* and *The Mansion* later. But why would Faulkner be less expensive than Isherwood? No matter. Now we had a choice. We could buy the less expensive Faulkner and put back the Isherwood.

Reluctantly, we started to put back the Isherwood.

"The Isherwood is a better buy," the dealer noted. "It was a much smaller printing."

"Oh."

"If you take both, I won't charge you tax," he said.

CHAPTER 8

The second Friday in November found us back in Boston. We had succeeded in whittling Claire down to $120 but only on the condition that we be back before noon the next day. "I got another job at one," she informed us.

We went to Boston with the express purpose of attending the Boston Antiquarian Book Fair. It was to be held, according to the circular we had picked up at the Book Fair in Sheffield, on Friday from 5:00 to 9:00, and Saturday and Sunday from 10:00 to 6:00.

We got to Boston early and decided to go see some of the stores in Back Bay that we had passed over the first time. The first place we went to was Avenue Victor Hugo down toward the end of Newbury Street.

We stopped in front of 339, a red brick building with a small storefront. There were two windows on either side of a door. The smaller window on the left held a display of old *Life* magazines. There was a smiling Donna Reed cover; a "Khrushchev Remembers World War II" issue with a picture of Khrushchev wrapped up in an enormous fur coat with a dopey hat on his head; Henry Fonda as "Mr. Roberts"; John Glenn in his space helmet; and a very young, very glamorous Paul Newman and Joanne Woodward. The window on the right held books and the signs:

<table>
<tr><td>AVENUE</td><td>NEW & USED</td></tr>
<tr><td>VICTOR HUGO</td><td>BOOKS</td></tr>
<tr><td>BOOKSHOP</td><td>MAGAZINES</td></tr>
<tr><td>EST. 1972</td><td>CARDS</td></tr>
<tr><td></td><td>BUY ★ TRADE ★ SELL</td></tr>
</table>

In many ways, Avenue Victor Hugo was precisely the sort of used-book store we had become used to in the Berkshires. The floors were old, as were the knocked-together shelves and there were masses of books. But, unlike Berkshire Book Company or Farshaw's, Avenue Victor Hugo was *hip*. The man behind the desk wore a sweatshirt and a baseball cap that were as old as most of the books and not in as good condition. When we checked our backpack (a requirement, not a courtesy), he gave us half of a tarot card and clipped the other half to the backpack with a clothespin. Instead of classical music, jazz from a local radio station floated through the store. A handmade sign read PLEASE HANDLE THE BOOKS.

The books that we were being encouraged to handle were clean and cheap; most were in the under-ten-dollar range. Up until about a month ago, we would happily have spent the greater part of the afternoon in Avenue Victor Hugo. As it was, we found a nice minor Le Carré and a later edition *Rebecca* by Daphne du Maurier. But, this trip, what we had really come to see were first editions.

There was a first-edition section to the left of the desk, but it started at the ceiling and came down to eye-level so you had to stand on a stepladder to see anything before the letter *T*. We searched eagerly but there was nothing there that interested us.

"Which one is next?" one of us asked the other as we stood on the sidewalk outside Avenue Victor Hugo ten minutes later consulting our trusty Yellow Pages photocopy.

"Buddenbrooks."

Buddenbrooks was listed on Boylston Street only about five minutes away. We hurried along until we reached the address on the sheet. It was a doughnut shop. We checked again and saw a door next to the shop with a list of tenants. There was a little sign that read BUDDEN-BROOKS HAS MOVED, and gave an address on Newbury Street that, given the confines of Back Bay, was also only about five minutes away.

The new location was on the second floor of one of those lovely brownstones that make Boston such a neat city. We walked up. The door at the top of the stairs was propped open. We stuck our heads in tentatively. There was no one in sight.

"Hello?"

At that, a man popped out of a side room. He was dressed in jeans. "Yes?" he said.

"Is this Buddenbrooks?"

"Well, yes," he said cheerfully, "but I'm afraid we're not open." He waved his arm and indicated the surrounding area. "We just moved. With the book fair and all, we haven't unpacked yet."

We looked around. The walls were lined with beautiful polished-glass-enclosed floor-to-ceiling bookcases, all completely empty.

"Oh. Does that mean there's nothing to look at?"

"Afraid so," said the man. He was about forty, medium height and thin, with brown hair and a beard. In his unpacking clothes, he looked more like a graduate student than the owner of a bookstore. "All I have out is what I'm taking to the fair. You going?"

"Yes, that's why we came. We were hoping to be able to look a little first, though."

"Sorry." The man shrugged. "But come by and see me at the fair. Or drop by in a week or two. We'll have everything ready to go by then. I'll even be able to offer you a cup of coffee or a hot chocolate."

Our next stop was David L. O'Neal Bookseller, Fine and Rare Books. This would be the very first time we had walked into a shop that specifically announced that it sold fine and rare books. O'Neal's was also on the second floor, in another brownstone, this one on a side street between Newbury and Commonwealth Avenue, two blocks up from Buddenbrooks.

This brownstone had a very classy lobby, recently renovated, mirrored and tiled in a soft aqua. The stairs to the second floor were carpeted and the wooden banister polished. Unlike Buddenbrooks, the door to O'Neal's was solid metal and locked. We had to press a buzzer for admittance.

A sandy-haired man in his thirties wearing a dark banker's suit and a maroon tie opened the door and paused in the doorway for just that moment that said we were being sized up. Then he stood aside stiffly and said, "Please come in."

The entire shop was one large rectangular room with six-foot-high bookshelves that ringed the perimeter. The shelves themselves were polished hardwood. Classical music played softly from unseen speakers and there were Oriental rugs on the floor. This was the first time that we had been in a bookshop where there were no free-standing bookshelves in the center. It made the room look empty.

Except for the music, O'Neal's had a hushed, museumlike quality. Although we were only one floor off the ground, we could not hear any street noise. Other than the man in the suit, who did not bother to introduce himself, there were only two other people in the shop, both middle-aged women who might have been either employees or customers.

The books on the shelves weren't like those in the other bookstores we'd seen, either. There were few dust jackets. Most of the books were bound in leather, they were all polished and appeared to be grouped by colors. Light reflected off the covers.

We weren't in the store a nanosecond before we realized that here, we were not buying anything.

The sandy-haired man stood nearby. "Were you looking for anything in particular, sir?" he asked. He spoke as if he were trying to keep his voice to a whisper, not unlike a junior associate at a funeral director's.

"Uh, modern firsts?" we replied, parroting the dealer at the book fair. It was the only phrase we knew. We felt like the immigrant who always eats the same thing because all he can say in English is "ham and eggs."

"We occasionally have some . . . of those," he said, pointing to the section nearest the door. He hesitated a moment. "Let me show you what we do here," he said finally. "We specialize in fine sets." He looked at us. "Do you know anything about binding?"

"Uh—"

"Well, we have the finest binders and illustrators," he said, proceeding to rattle off a bunch of names we'd never heard of and frankly don't remember. He picked up a book. It was one of six. The book was bound in a rich dark green leather. He opened the book. We only recognized one word on the page: "Goethe." The rest was in German. We did see one other thing as well. It was on a little piece of paper, typed or printed (in English), that lay between the cover and the endpaper. On it was a description of the set and presumably what it was, although the sandy-haired man turned the page too quickly for us to read it. The price was also on the piece of paper and that we did spot. It was sixty-five hundred dollars.

As quickly as he opened the book, he closed it. "Dickens is over here, the other English writers are over here, the French are over here . . ." He indicated a couple of other sections. Then he said abruptly, "If you need any help, sir, let me know," turned on his heel, and strode away, leaving us standing there in the middle of the floor.

Our next stop was to be Pepper and Stern, just around the corner on Boylston Street. Pepper and Stern also advertised itself as a rare-book dealer. After O'Neal's, we were a little shy about going in.

We finally decided to chance it and hiked up the stairs to the inevitable second floor. We turned to the left and walked in an open door.

If O'Neal's was a mortuary, Pepper and Stern was a fire drill in a kindergarten. It was a small room, but people were everywhere, standing, talking animatedly in small knots, moving in and out of the door or loading books onto little rolling carts and scurrying off. No one paid the least bit of attention to us.

Finally, we stopped a man in his late twenties who appeared from his frantic activity and the fact that he was carrying an armload of books to have some association with the place. He was wearing blue jeans, a white T-shirt, a black studded belt and penny loafers. His hair was cut short and slicked so that little clumps stuck up like porcupine bristles everywhere except in the front where it was slicked together flat as a table, forty-five degrees to the vertical.

"Are you open?" we asked idiotically.

"Yes," he replied breathlessly, "but we're getting ready for the fair."

"That's why we came to town. But we were hoping to see something first."

"Cool. Look around." He spoke breathlessly even when he wasn't moving. He turned but we stopped him.

"What are these?" We were standing in front of a very tall bookshelf filled with what appeared to be mysteries. But they all had unusual covers. "Is this the mystery section?"

"No, Peter collects art deco dust jackets." This response was not altogether helpful since we had no idea who Peter was.

"Who's Peter?"

"He's the Stern."

"Are you the Pepper?"

"No. He's in California. I'm the Brian." He was about to start away again, then stopped. "Are you interested in anything in particular?"

"Modern firsts?"

"Right around here," Brian said instantly, zipping around to a little alcove formed by the back side of the bookcase that held the art deco covers. "These," he said, pointing to a rolling cart with three shelves, filled with books, "are the ones we're taking to the fair. You can't buy them. Well, you can but not here. I suppose you could if you really wanted to . . ."

"That's all right."

"Now these," Brian went on, sweeping his hand up and down

a packed thirty-six square feet of bookcase, "these you can buy. They're staying here. If you need anything, give a whistle." Then, as if in a puff of smoke, he was gone.

The first thing we noticed about the section at which Brian had left us was how very appealing it looked, all the different colors from all those different dust jackets. And there were so many. We went first to writers we knew. John Le Carré, for example. There were about six of them but the one that stood out was *The Spy Who Came in from the Cold*. "First UK," it said in pencil on the front endpaper, "$900." *From Here to Eternity*. A first edition in perfect condition. That was $450. A step in the right direction. *For Whom the Bell Tolls*. $350. There were lots of P. G. Wodehouse, all in the $150 to $250 range.

All the while we were looking, we could peripherally see blurred images of young men and women sprinting back and forth. We heard the indistinct buzz of voices and the sound of ringing telephones. It was more like a Wall Street trading room than a bookstore. If the books had been any less intoxicating, we would have merely stood on the side of the room and watched the action.

We wanted to buy a book from Pepper and Stern.

We looked and looked but even their mediocre books were a good deal more expensive than *Nineteen Eighty-four*, our most expensive book. *Paths of Glory*, by Humphrey Cobb, for example, a book whose only claim to fame was that it had been made into a brilliant film by Stanley Kubrick, was $250.

By the time we got to Steinbeck, we were forlorn. Then we pulled out a copy of *The Winter of Our Discontent*. *The Winter of Our Discontent* is a nice little book. It's not *Of Mice and Men* or *The Grapes of Wrath*, of course, but still it's Steinbeck and it was . . . thirty-five dollars.

"We'll take this one," we said to Brian.

"Very good," he said, not at all judgmental even though it was clear that we were buying the least expensive book in the entire shop.

He disappeared for a few moments and then returned with a computer-generated invoice.

We signed the credit card slip, took the book that Brian had carefully wrapped in brown paper, and told him that we would see him at the fair.

"Make sure and get there early tomorrow," said Brian. "A lot of the best books go in the first hour."

"Oh, we have to leave tomorrow. We're going tonight."

"But you can't go tonight," said Brian, looking aghast.

"Why not?"

"Tonight's session isn't open to the public. It's only for dealers."

"It can't be." We whipped out the little "Boston Antiquarian Book Fair" card that we had picked up at the book fair in Sheffield. "Here." We pointed to the part that read "Friday 5–9." "This doesn't say anything about not being open to the public."

Brian examined the card. He even turned it over once or twice. "Maybe they changed it," he said finally.

"How can we find out?"

"You can call." There was a telephone number on the card.

"May we use your phone?"

Brian glanced at the phones, each of which seemed to ring the second the receiver was replaced.

"If you can find one," he said.

After about five minutes, we got to call the book fair.

"Is tonight's session open to the public?"

"No," answered a harried man on the other end, "it's only open to members of the trade and exhibitors."

"It doesn't say that on the card."

"Yes, I know," replied the man apologetically. "We've been having a lot of trouble about that."

He was having trouble. "We drove in all the way from Lenox. Since the card is wrong, could we come tonight just to look?"

"Afraid not," said the man. "Can't you come tomorrow morning? We're open at ten."

We considered the consequences of keeping Claire waiting while she was alone with our child. "Afraid not."

When we got off the phone, we were surprised to see Brian standing just behind us.

"How did you make out?"

"They're not going to let us in."

"I didn't think they would," he said. "Book dealers are notoriously inflexible." Then he paused for a moment, running something through his head. He seemed genuinely sympathetic. He went to the desk. Was he going to give us a badge or something that identified us as dealers so we could go to the private preview? He turned back and handed us a small book.

"Here," he said. "Take a copy of our catalogue."

So, while everyone in the book world was at the dealers-only preview, we made the best of it with some great sushi and returned to our hotel room at the Eliot (we were learning) to climb into our big, cushy king-size bed and, among other things, look through our new books.

The first book we looked through was the Pepper and Stern catalogue.

And we thought the shop had been impressive.

It became clear in the first two or three pages that Brian had not showed us everything. Every book we had been looking for was here.

Want a good hard-boiled mystery?

CAIN, JAMES M. *The Postman Always Rings Twice.* New York: Alfred A. Knopf, 1934. First Edition. Very light spotting of the edges, corner of the first couple of pages creased, a fine copy in a dust jacket with a little rubbing of the extremities. A remarkably clean and solid copy of a book that is highly prone to shaking.

Accompanied by the original design for the jacket spine and front cover, signed at the bottom, "The original jacket design by Philip Van Doren Stern." The finished dust jacket has some differences, mostly in the placement of the author's name, but the basic design is the same, with pencilled dimensions and notes in the margins.

$5,000.00

Oh, and *The Hamlet*. We'd been looking for that one, too.

FAULKNER, WILLIAM. *The Hamlet*. New York: Random House, 1940. First Edition. Near fine in a very good dust jacket.

Signed on the title page, "William Faulkner, Oxford, Miss, 27 June, 1941." Inscribed by Faulkner on the fly-leaf with a private joke, "With love to Abe from Gertrude."

$10,000.00

And *Dracula*. There were two of those.

STOKER, BRAM. *Dracula*. London: Archibald Constable, 1897. First Edition, first printing, first issue. Front hinge cracking, back hinge just barely started, small cloth tears at the top and bottom of the spine, light foxing and minor soiling. Overall, on the objective scale, a very good copy. On the subjective scale, given the fragility of the book's manufacture, and the tendency of the book to attract soiling, much better than usual. Much better copies rarely turn up, and later issues and printings are often sold (usually innocently) as firsts. The later printing is on a smooth, thinner paper, thus the book is noticeably slimmer, and there is clear type deterioration. This copy, like copies inscribed on publication day has no publisher's advertisements at all. Later issues may have one page (including Stoker's *Shoulder of Shasta*), or several pages, some even advertising *Dracula*.

$9,500.00

If $9,500 was too steep, you could always step down to:

STOKER, BRAM. *Dracula*. New York: Doubleday
& McClure, 1899. First American Edition. Tiny spot on
front cover, minute wear, a fine copy.

$4,000.00

There was Stephen Crane's *Red Badge of Courage* for $6,500,
Raymond Chandler's *Big Sleep* for $8,500, and Ayn Rand's own copy
of *The Fountainhead* for $15,000. *The Grapes of Wrath* was here, as was
George Orwell, Sinclair Lewis, and H. P. Lovecraft (the original page
proofs to *The Outsider and Others* for $15,000). The descriptions were
filled with words like "foxing," "bubbling," "rubbing," "chipped"
and, provocatively, "cocked." Hinges might be "cracking" or "just
starting." Some books had "boards," others had "wrappers." "Fine"
seemed to have a special meaning—there was "fine," "near fine,"
"about fine" and "very fine." Then there was "good" and "very
good." The only thing that we were sure we understood was the sym-
bol "$."

Not everything was in the $5,000 to $15,000 range, of course.
If we wanted to move out of the cheap stuff, there was a *Gulliver's
Travels,* first edition, first printing, portrait in second state (whatever
that meant) for $47,500.

And then there was the most expensive item of all. It wasn't
Dickens, it wasn't Shakespeare, it wasn't Voltaire, Molière, or Mark
Twain. Nor was it a great contemporary writer like Fitzgerald or
Hemingway. It was:

BURROUGHS, EDGAR RICE. *Tarzan of the
Apes*. Chicago: A.C. McClurg, 1914. First Edition, first
printing, first binding. Minutely used, a fine copy in a fine
dust jacket. In a full morocco case.

The inside of the dust jacket has the ownership signature and notes of the author's son, Hulbert Burroughs,

who well-meaningly put tape around the inside along the edges and folds. This tape has been removed without damage. Truly a beautiful copy of a rare book. The last copy in dust jacket sold at auction was at the Bradley Martin sale, which brought $26,400.00, was a second binding, the jacket of which was worn and browned at the edges, and with a long scratch in the front panel (enthusiastically described in the catalogue as "a fine copy").

First appearing in the magazine *All-Story* in 1912, the character of Tarzan appeared in Burroughs' own sequels, movies, television, comic books, a successful comic strip and spin-off products. Burroughs was the first writer of fiction to shrewdly exploit his creation in a manner which is now considered business as usual. As a matter of fact, Tarzan was the first literary character to be registered as a trademark. He created his own publishing and marketing company, E.R.B., Inc., located in Tarzana, California, which is the only example that comes to mind of a town named after a fictional character.

$50,000.00

Fifty thousand dollars for *Tarzan*? You could buy your own jungle for that. Could it be that somehow *Tarzan* was great literature and we didn't know it? Was the book made of gold?

What was going on here, anyway?

CHAPTER 9

*I*t was Thanksgiving, two weeks after the Boston Antiquarian Book Fair that we did not get to attend. We were in Chicago, on another family trip.

We had left our daughter with her grandparents and hotfooted it into Chicago to have lunch at the glorified diner with the amazing French toast and shirred eggs and visit the same bookstores we'd been to on the last trip.

We were at Rohe, wandering around in the Literature section. With the Steinbeck's was a copy of *The Moon Is Down*.

The Moon Is Down was published just after the United States entered World War II, and is the story of the Nazi occupation of a small coal-mining town. It is written from the point of view of both the occupiers and the occupied and is sympathetic to each. The German force is led by Colonel Lanser, a polite, educated, and sensitive man who attempts to be fair and respect the occupants of the town that he has come to as an invader. The town is led by Mayor Orden, still referred to in the traditional manner as "Your Excellency."

A tacit agreement is struck between two reasonable men. The

Germans will allow the town to function, within limits, as closely as possible to the way it did before the occupation, if there is no resistance. Accordingly, the majority of the German soldiers conduct themselves in a civilized manner, extending respect and even politeness to the inhabitants. The townspeople, for their part, go about their business, ignoring the occupiers.

Then the bargain falls apart.

Unlike *The Winter of Our Discontent,* which is a nice little book, *The Moon Is Down* is, in our opinion, a great little book. It is powerful and heart-rending in its simplicity, and the characterizations are uniformly, achingly real.

We looked through the book. It had no dust jacket but, from the copyright page, it appeared that it might be a first edition. The price was five dollars.

We took it to the desk. "Is this a first edition?" we asked the young man behind the desk.

He looked at the book. "Yes," he said. "But it's second state and it doesn't have a dust jacket so what it is basically is a very nice reading copy."

So we bought it.

Later that afternoon, on our last stop of the day, we went to Titles, in Highland Park.

Titles was a small, cozy antiquarian bookshop on a side street, close to a jeweler and a furrier, which will give you a sense of what Highland Park is like. Not much larger than a good-size living room and considerably narrower, Titles' stock was small but well presented. At the front of the store on the left was American History with the emphasis on regional stuff, local history, Lincoln, that kind of thing. To the right were children's books and art books. In the middle were tables upon which were heaped sets and more art books and boxes containing old prints.

The entire back half of the shop was devoted to fiction. Along the left-hand wall were used books, everything from Stephen King to Evelyn Waugh. There were a lot of P. G. Wodehouse and

E. Phillips Oppenheim. Not everything had a dust jacket, and there were a lot of minor books, but they were all in very good shape and most were protected with plastic. Along the right-hand wall were first editions.

At the back of the shop was a desk at which sat a well-dressed woman in her midfifties. She was speaking on the telephone in an animated fashion when we walked in and made no move to stop at the sight of customers.

Titles turned out to be a terrific store for us. Like Pepper and Stern, it was one of those places where even the books we weren't interested in looked interesting.

On the first-edition side (where we were) were signed copies of everything T. Coraghessan Boyle ever wrote, Ian Fleming and James Clavell but also Upton Sinclair and some Mark Twains (although not *Huckleberry Finn* or *Tom Sawyer*). Almost immediately we saw two books we wanted to have: *The Jungle,* Upton Sinclair's savage attack on the inhuman conditions endured by immigrant workers in the Chicago meatpacking industry at the turn of the century and *The Member of the Wedding,* Carson McCullers's coming of age novel.

We took down the books and approached the woman behind the desk. She was just wrapping up her telephone conversation. Behind her, on the wall, was an autographed photo of Paul Newman, the kind you usually see in restaurants or dry cleaners, which was inscribed "To Florence. Best Wishes."

"Hi, Florence."

Florence blinked behind her glasses. "Do I know you?" she asked, with the trace of an accent that was definitely not Midwestern.

We pointed toward the picture.

"Ah." She laughed.

"Is he a collector?"

"No," she said. "I just love him."

"You're not from around here, are you? Originally, I mean."

"Brooklyn," she said.

"Me, too. What high school did you go to?"

"Tilden. I didn't talk to anybody for four years. My parents moved. My sister got to stay at Erasmus."

"Erasmus was my district school. But I went to Stuyvesant."

"Isn't that a science school?" asked Florence, peering with surprise.

"Don't I look like the type?"

"No," she said, declining to elaborate further. The telephone began to ring again. Florence made no move to answer.

"Don't you have to get that?"

"No, that's my personal line. I usually let it ring. When I don't pick it up, my family thinks I'm lying dead somewhere."

"So if I don't look like I belonged in a science school, what do I look like?"

She thought for a minute. "You look like a writer," she said.

"How did you know? Did someone tell you we were coming?"

"You really are a writer? Who are you?"

"I'm Larry Goldstone and this is my wife, Nancy. She's a writer, too."

There was a moment of uncomfortable silence that we had encountered before.

"Don't worry, Florence. There's no reason you would have ever heard of either of us."

"It doesn't matter," she said. "Reputations go up and down. I know Joseph Heller . . . I read *Something Happened* and I liked it . . . almost nobody else did . . . it touched something . . . I recognized something about myself." Florence laughed. "I told that to my friend and she said, 'You must be a horrible person.' Anyway, I wrote to him after I finished the book and he wrote me back a lovely reply. After that, we corresponded a little. Later on, he came to Chicago for a signing . . . it was so sad. Dick Francis was in a store nearby and the lines were around the block. It got so bad that the bookstore had to tell people two books only . . . you know, people were bringing everything they had of his for him to sign. And he's written so many books.

"They had rented a theater for Heller and only about fifty people showed up. He was sitting there at a table and I came up with all my books. When I told him who I was, he stood, came around, and gave me a hug and kiss. It was so sweet."

"It must be terrible, having your first book do so well and then, afterward, nothing. And it was more than a book . . . *Catch-22* was the statement of a generation."

Florence nodded. "Sometimes I think that the only writers who make it are the ones with the big personalities," she said. "Some terrific writers are so inarticulate. Nelson Algren was like that . . . we were friends with him and one night, when he came to dinner, he sat at the table and didn't say a word the whole night. Then, after dinner, he walked over to the typewriter, sat down and knocked off a paragraph. It was fabulous. I thought, 'Where does this come from?' "

We talked a little more, then paid for *The Jungle* and *The Member of the Wedding*. The telephone rang. We looked at Florence.

"This is the business line," she said, picking it up.

On the way out, walking past the first-edition section, we happened to look down and, on the bottom shelf, just off the floor, we saw *The Moon Is Down*.

We immediately bent over and pulled it out. It had a dust jacket enclosed in a plastic sleeve, and seemed to be in very good condition. We opened the front cover and, on a little piece of white printed paper, we read:

Steinbeck, John. *The Moon Is Down* New York: Viking, 1942. First edition, first state with "talk.this" on page 112. Fine in a near fine dust jacket. $150.

The man behind the counter at Rohe had said "no dust jacket, second state." And now here was a dust jacket and a first state. Obviously, the presence of the dust jacket and the earlier state (whatever a state was) accounted for a $145 difference in price.

Our first reaction was that, for five dollars, we had gotten the better deal. Our second reaction was that our first reaction was undoubtedly wrong.

"What does first state mean?"

We were back in Massachusetts, talking to David.

"First styte? It's the paht of the first printing before they find the mistykes."

"Mistakes?"

"Roight. Sometime during the printing run, the publisher notices that there was a mistyke . . . I think I can show you roight here . . . let's see."

He walked over to the first-edition section and withdrew two copies of *For Whom the Bell Tolls.* On one copy, the dust jacket was torn and missing a piece at the top. On the other, the dust jacket was crisp and bright.

"All roight," he said. "Which is the better copy?"

Both of us pointed to the cleaner dust jacket although we both knew that it must be the wrong answer.

"Wrong," said David, turning them over. Hemingway's picture covered the back cover, except for a red border on the bottom with "Ernest Hemingway" in script. "Now look at the two covers and tell me what's different."

We stared for a few moments, feeling like two kids flunking a game of "What's wrong with this picture?" then gave up.

"Look at the bottom, on the border," David prompted.

Then we saw it.

"Roight," he said. "The photographer's signature is on the clean dust jacket but not on the worn one."

"And it should be," we said.

"Roight. In the first styte, they left it out. It was a mistyke. A clean copy of the first styte would be about two hundred fifty dollars, sometimes a lot more."

"How much is this one?"

David checked inside. It read "1st DJ, but book is later printing. $35."

"How do you know it's a later printing?"

David opened the book to the copyright page. "Scribner's always put an 'A' below the copyroight information in their first editions." There was no "A."

"Okay," we said, "we'll take it anyway."

"All roight. Interested in points now, are you?"

"Points?"

"Points of issue. That's what they call the errors that separate one styte or issue from another."

"We saw *The Moon Is Down* in Chicago."

"Oh, yes. That's the one with the period in the middle of the sentence, isn't it? Remember the pyge, by chance?"

The page? "No," we replied.

David went to his desk, opened the drawer, and took out a little orange book that said "Points of Issue" on top. "If you want to be really precoise, you have to check BAL . . . that's *Bibliography of American Literature* . . . or another good bibliography, but in a pinch, these little books do quoite noicely. You should buy a set if you're going to go to book fairs." He leafed through the pages. "Yes, here it is . . ."

He held out the book and showed us the entry. It read:

STEINBECK, John. *THE MOON IS DOWN.*
New York, 1942. CP: No Printer's name 112.11: talk.this

"That means that the nyme of the printer is on the copyroight pyge of the lyter issues but not on the first and that on pyge one hundred twelve, loine eleven, there's a period in the middle of a sentence that shouldn't be there and isn't there in the other printings.

"There's another one of these books that shows you how to identify first editions," David went on, "loike the 'A' in the Scribners. A fellow by the nyme of Bill McBroide puts them out. He's in Connecticut. I'll give you the telephone number before you go. Also, if you're going to staht playing around with this stuff, first editions and all, you should read up a little."

"Any recommendations?" we asked.

"Sure. Wyte here." David left the shop and disappeared into the house. When he returned, he was carrying an armload of books. "Here," he said. "You can borrow these. Some are better than others, but just about anything you want to know is in one or another of them."

David gave us seven books in all. We took them home and pored through each with a mixture of an aficionado's enthusiasm and a high school student's irritation.

We realized almost immediately that all seven were basically the same book written in slightly different ways (hopefully by slightly different people). The only variations seemed to be in the organization and in the competition for the cleverest chapter headings and the driest prose. In the chapter heading category, the winner was *A Primer of Book Collecting,* by John T. Winterich and David A. Randall (Bell, 1966). *Primer* was divided into two sections, "The Quarry," and "The Chase," and among the chapter headings were "First Editions and Blood Relations," and "What Makes a Rare Book Rare?" Dry prose went to *Modern Book Collecting* by Robert A. Wilson (Lyons & Burford, 1980), which could have been very useful to us in that it focused primarily on modern firsts, but unfortunately relied on sentences such as:

> It will be noted that more and more American publishers are adopting a system of ascending numbers printed on the copyright page, sometimes along with the words "First Edition." These words and the numeral "1" are then removed from the plate at the time of the seond printing so that the number series now begins with "2".

Book Collecting: A Comprehensive Guide by Allen Ahearn (Putnam, 1989) seemed to be the least useful of all. It was 320 pages long of which 204 pages simply listed the first books of more than thirty-five hundred authors and their "estimated value." (Why first books, we had no idea.) Of the other 116 pages, 55 were devoted to appendices and more lists of bibliophile esoterica. The remaining 61 pages contained some useful information, although roughly the same stuff found in the other six books. Why anyone would pay over twenty dollars for a book such as this was completely beyond us.

Two of the books were actually nothing more than oversize, annotated lists. *The List of Books: A Library of over 3,000 Works* by Frederic Raphael and Kenneth McLeish (Harmony, 1981) was . . . a list of books and *ABC for Book-Collectors,* by John Carter (Grenada Publishing Limited, sixth edition, reprinted 1985) was a list of terms. The three thousand works in *The List of Books* covered everything from fiction to anthropology to home and garden to sex and love.

ABC was actually a handy book to have around, being literally an A to Z listing of apparently every term ever used by book collectors. If we ever wanted to know what "tree-calf" or a "point-maniac" was, this was the place to look.

Flawed as many of them were individually, taken as a group the books provided a solid foundation for what was previously only guesswork on our part. With *ABC* at our elbow, we were finally able to decipher Pepper and Stern's catalogue, with its "foxed" and "rubbed" and "backstrip" and "joints." For example, "foxed" was:

Of paper: discolored, stained, usually with brownish-yellowish spots. Foxing is due to chemical action in paper which has been badly bleached in manufacture, usually caused by damp or lack of ventilation. Some authorities derive the term (first noted in 1848) from the color of the spots: most are silent on its origin.

"Rubbed" was:

Rubbed and its polite synonym *chafed* are the equivalent of what the French call *fatigué.* If the BACKSTRIP or the JOINTS of a copy are described in the catalogue as *rubbed,* they will not necessarily be weak, but they are probably well on their way to it; and if the binding is of leather, they will be in need of resuscitation.

The "backstrip" was the spine and the "joints" were the hinges. The varying degrees of "fine" and "good" turned out to be points along the line of description of condition. "Excellent" was best, next comes "very fine," then "fine," followed by "near fine" or "about fine" then "very good" and "good." (Or, as Brian at Pepper and Stern told us later, "In this business, good is not good.")

It took us two weeks but we finally plowed through all seven. At the time, it seemed to be a lot of work just to be able to buy something to read.

We had called Bill McBride as David had suggested and ordered the two little books. The woman who answered said that they were putting out updated editions in a few weeks, so we ordered the new ones. About a month later our *Pocket Guide to the Identification of First Editions* and *Points of Issue* arrived in the mail.

We immediately began checking out books we knew. Under Hemingway was listed:

FOR WHOM THE BELL TOLLS, New York, 1940
DJ: back panel: photo lacks photographer's name underneath.

We checked *The Moon Is Down* and the "talk.this" was listed on page 112.

Now we were real collectors.

We continued to leaf through the books until eventually we came to Faulkner. There it was:

FAULKNER, William. *THE TOWN.* New York, 1957.
     Trade Edition. B: red cloth TE: grey EP: grey patterned   327.8&10 repeated

We checked our own edition of *The Town,* the one we had purchased at the book fair in Sheffield for sixty dollars, the one that had read "1st Edition."

The binding was orange cloth, not red.

The top edge was green, not gray.

The endpapers were uncolored, not gray patterned.

Hey, wait a minute. On page 327, line 8 *was* repeated on line 10. Still, in this game, one out of four was not good enough.

We didn't have a real first edition, after all.

Damn.

CHAPTER 10

One afternoon in mid-April, we were in Farshaw's, chatting with Helen.

"Are you coming to the auction?" she asked.

Before we could ask, "What auction?" Helen had taken a small card off a stack at the side of the counter and handed it to us:

Berkshire Book Auction.
Sale 10: A Fine Assortment of Rare Books.
Monday, April 24, 1995, at 6:30 P.M.
The American Legion Hall.
Route 7, Sheffield, Ma.

While we were still looking at the card, she said, "It's a terrific auction. There'll be some very interesting items. I think you should go."

It sounded like a neat idea. Neither of us had ever attended an auction before.

"Would you like a catalogue?" she asked, reaching to another stack. She handed us a small gray pamphlet. "These are usually five dollars but you can have this one."

We looked at the pamphlet. On the cover was the same information that appeared on the card, but there was also an illustration of weird animals that looked like a cross between *Alice in Wonderland* and *Jurassic Park*. It was from lot 179, Soldini, *De Anima Brutorum* (Florence, 1776).

"There'll be a lot of contemporary items, too," she said. "You'll probably want to bid."

"Yes, maybe," we replied. "Who runs this?"

"We do," she said. "Berkshire Book Auction is one of our other businesses. This is our second year. It's going very well. This one is going to be our best one yet. We have some wonderful books this time."

"How do you get your books?"

"Oh, people come to us. You know, we often act as agent for people trying to sell collections of their private papers to libraries."

"Really."

"Yes. That's another one of our businesses. Michael is very well known. People have contacted us from all over the world. He's handled the papers of some very important people."

"Like who?"

"Well, we're not really supposed to say. Most of the people Michael represents don't want anyone to know that they're selling their papers. They think that it makes them look kind of mercenary." Then she lowered her voice and proceeded to whisper the name of one of the world's best-known playwrights.

The American Legion Hall was a one-story, white vinyl-sided building, about thirty feet by fifty, with the obligatory cannon and flagpole out front. There were also two signs sitting on the lawn: BOOK AUCTION, MONDAY, 6:30, and KIWANIS LAS VEGAS NIGHT, MAY 20TH.

The interior of the American Legion Hall consisted of one large room with adjoining bathrooms and kitchen. The walls were paneled in a pale yellowish brown, fake-wood laminate with painted (although not recently) concrete floors and the kind of metal folding chairs you find in the emergency rooms of bad hospitals. Dirty burnt orange curtains hung resolutely over undersize windows. There were a number of bulletins posted on the wall, but our eyes were immediately drawn to:

AMERICAN LEGION POST 340

FUNERAL DETAIL

ELIGIBILITY DATES (WWI, WWII, KOREA, VIETNAM)

NEW ELIGIBILITY DATES (GRENADA/LEBANON, PANAMA,

PERSIAN GULF)

The kitchen was large and institutional with stainless steel everywhere. We looked inside and thought cholesterol. An open package of doughnuts sat on the counter that separated the kitchen from the main room, two remaining unclaimed from the original twelve. It was unclear whether it was tonight's participants or some previous group that had devoured the other ten.

At Helen's suggestion, we had arrived about an hour early for the preview. A double row of long brown Formica tables had been set up along the south side of the room to accommodate the over two hundred lots that made up the auction. Each lot had a numbered white index card sitting neatly in front of it, identifying its place in the order of items to be bid on. About fifty people were already there, milling around the room, a few of whom we knew. Most of the browsers were obviously dealers. There was an overrepresentation of beards, checked shirts, and baseball hats. The feel was vaguely agricultural except that everyone was wearing glasses.

Esther had come (although not David), as had Bob and Bonnie Benson from Yellow House, and Bruce Gventer. Although everyone seemed to know one another, no one spoke, except for some occasional snippets of forced conversation. The dealers walked up and down the aisles, examining the lots, making quick, surreptitious notes in catalogues or notebooks.

Even Esther was not as we had come to know her.

"Hi, Esther," we said, smiling.

"Oh," she replied, appearing startled. "Hello." She closed her notebook.

"Are you going to bid?"

"Oh, there might be one or two things," she replied, glancing furtively from side to side.

"Which ones?"

"Oh, there might be one or two things," she repeated vaguely, moving off.

Although Sale 10 was billed as a "rare book" auction, there was an extraordinary variety of other items on which to bid. There were hundreds of volumes, both individual and in sets but we also saw old maps, illustrated plates, cartoon cels, Soviet propaganda sketches, theatrical playbills, obscure magazines, atom bomb memorabilia, and a folder of letters from the files of a Hollywood business manager that included "a most provocative ALS (autographed letter, signed) from Elizabeth Taylor." The books themselves were equally diverse. Everything from a 1795 copy of *The Poems of William Shakespeare* to a first edition of Mark Twain's *A Tramp Abroad* to *Gertrude of Wyoming: A Pennsylvanian Tale* to the 1830 edition of *Papyro-Plastics, or the Art of Modeling in Paper. Being an Instructive Amusement for Young Persons of Both Sexes*. From the German.

There was quite a bit of Americana. The Berkshires is known for its Americana. "Ana" has a very specific meaning to bibliophiles. We knew because we had looked it up in *ABC for Book-Collectors*. It said that "ana" was:

A collective noun meaning a compilation of sayings, table talk, anecdotes, etc. Southey described Boswell's *Johnson* as "the Ana of all Anas." Its most familiar use is, however, the original one (from which the noun was made) in the form of a Latin suffix, meaning material relating to as distinct from material by; e.g. Boswelliana, Railroadiana,

Etoniana. Like other such suffixes it is not always easily attachable to English names, even assisted, as commonly, by a medial *i*. Shaviana, Harveiana and Dickensiana are well enough; but Hardyana is repugnant to Latinity; and should one write Wiseiana, Wiseana or Wisiana?

We hypothesized from all this that Americana is anything *about* America as opposed to anything written *by* an American. We had no idea who Wise was.

Americana, therefore, took in a lot of territory. At this auction, for example, *Acts Passed at the Third Congress of the United States of America,* was Americana, as was *Gertrude of Wyoming,* but Mark Twain was not. Or maybe he was. To tell the truth, we weren't sure. All these specifics made things very vague.

When we had gone through the catalogue at home, we actually had seen something on which we might want to bid. It was lot 100:

100. Folio Society: *Dickens Novels and Dickens Encyclope-dia.* London, 1977–89. Original cloth and decorated boards, and slipcases, in near-fine condition. 17 vols.

$150–200

This looked like a fabulous opportunity. Dickens was one of our favorites and here was a chance to get either a complete set or close to a complete set of his work for as little as $150 or even less.

The lots were arranged in order of bidding and we walked down the table until we found the pile of books labeled lot 100. As advertised, each of the seventeen volumes was bound in a dark, almost hunter green cloth, the covers were decorated, and each was in its own dark green slipcase. ("Boards," by the way, in this case meant that the covers were made from cardboard as opposed to leather, not that they were slabs of wood.)

We took out *Oliver Twist* and examined it. The paper had body, the illustrations were quite nice and the book was in excellent condition. In fact, it did not look as if anyone had ever opened it before. But the second we looked at it, we knew we didn't want the set. The books were somehow too . . . *new*. Dickens should be . . . *old*. For people who love Dickens, part of the joy is being transported back to nineteenth-century London. You can almost feel the city around you when you read him, hear the clatter of hoofbeats on the cobblestones, feel your breath choked by the smoke and soot in the air. To have such a new, essentially utilitarian set as the representative of Charles Dickens in our library felt like sacrilege.

The only other item in the catalogue that had drawn our interest was lot 67:

67. Clemens, Samuel [Mark Twain]: *Life on the Mississippi*. First edition, First state. Boston, 1883. Original pictorial cloth, gilt edges (with the urn on p. 441 and "St. Louis Hotel" on p. 443). Shaken; some slightly splotchy fading to top cover and spine; bottom cover stained and bubbled, inner gutter cracked, marginal tears from p. 481–550. ARTHUR SWANN'S COPY, with his bookplate and pencilled notations on front pastedown, and a typed bibliographical note (2pp.) asserting that probably not more than 100 copies were printed with this presentation binding.

$200–250

Upon examination however, the book proved mostly to be a teaching aid in the terms used in all those books to describe flaws. "Shaken," for example, meant that the book was no longer firmly attached to its covers, "bubbled" that the cloth on the cover had partially detached from the boards. In other words, the book was in terrible shape. We certainly weren't going to pay two hundred dollars for a book that was falling apart.

All the same, we were disappointed. Now that we were here, we wanted to bid on something. To bid successfully, actually. We wandered a little bit down the table and our attention was drawn to a small pile of cream-colored books with delicate ornate gold script lettering and the kind of olive green flower pattern you see on Laura Ashley bedspreads. The little white card at the top read lot 91. We consulted the catalogue.

> 91. [Dulac]: *The Novels of the Sisters Brontë.* 10 vols. London, 1905. Orig. Illust. cloth. One or two covers a little worn/soiled. With six color plates by Dulac.

We looked at the books. "A little worn/soiled" was something of an understatement. They were, in fact, dirty. In addition, some of the covers were torn along the spines. Still, they weren't *that* dirty and it was a charming set, just right for the Brontës. The colored illustrations by Dulac (whoever he was) were wonderful.

The catalogue provided an estimated value of each lot. The most expensive was lot 179, Soldini, Francesco Maria: *De Anima Brutorum Comentaria,* a beautiful, engraved first edition of the Florentine book on vegetarianism printed in 1776, valued at $3,500 to $4,000. It was this book that had been the source of the cover illustration on the catalogue. The Brontë set that we were now looking at was listed at $30 to $60.

We spent a little more time browsing, then looked up at the clock. There was still almost half an hour before the auction was scheduled to begin.

We went outside. It was unusually warm for late April in the Berkshires. People were in shirtsleeves instead of ski jackets, probably for the first time in five months. The sky was cloudless and brilliantly blue. It was that time in late afternoon when the shadows were long but you could still feel the sun on your skin. Many of the dealers had also finished their inspections, moved outside, and were now chatting amiably in small groups. Most were eating. They were as collegial out here as they had been stealthy going up and down the aisles.

Michael was standing just outside the door in animated discussion with two other dealers. One of them was sitting on the ground with his back against the wall eating salad out of an aluminum container and the other was standing and eating a hot dog with a variety of condiments dripping out the sides. Michael was expounding on how the University of Texas, where he apparently had placed some papers, had used oil and cattle money to establish one of the premier libraries in the country.

We stood for a moment, not knowing in which direction to walk, feeling like we had just arrived at a cocktail party where we didn't know anyone except the host. So we walked up to the host.

We didn't expect much. Michael had always been a little distant with us. But now he was expansive and charming.

"Hello. Lovely to see you. How good of you to come," he said, immediately including us in his group. He leaned forward a little and again addressed the dealer sitting against the wall, giving us a sideways mischevious grin. "I brought one of the lots out here with me. Can you tell me where it is?"

The dealer looked up from his salad. "Give me a hint," he said.

Michael leaned a little farther over. "I'm the hint," he said.

"You stuffed something in your shirt," said the dealer.

"No," said Michael. "I'm wearing it."

"Oh," said the dealer. "The medallion."

"Correct!" said Michael, lifting a little medallion that he was wearing on a chain around his neck. He leaned down to give the dealer a closer look, then stood up and turned so we could see it. "Lot one seventy-five," he said.

We looked at it. It was small and appeared to be a silver coin with a picture of William Shakespeare on it. While Michael continued his discussion, we checked in the catalogue:

175. [Shakespeare—Jubilee Medal]: Silver medallion, approx. 1 1/4˝ in diameter with a relief portrait on the obverse of Shakespeare circumscribed by the words, "we shall not look upon his like again". The reverse has the words "Jubilee at Stratford in honour and to the memory of Shakespeare. Sept 1769 D.G. Steward". The medal was designed by David Garrick, the portrait was executed

by David Piper, and the medals were struck by Westwood of Birmingham. The medals were worn by guests and townspeople at the Shakespeare Jubilee festivities in Stratford organized by Garrick.

$600–750

Wow. We asked to see the medallion again. Michael leaned our way to let us see it but he was already off on another subject.

"We have some genuinely unique items this time," he was saying. "We're beginning to get calls from everywhere. Next time, we're going to have the entire stock of the old Raven bookshop in New York. And we've just finished placing a set of private papers at a major library."

"Whose?" asked the dealer with the hot dog.

Michael smiled and without the slightest hesitation repeated the name of the same world-famous playwright.

Now that we had determined that we were going to bid, it became necessary to figure out how to do it. We went back inside and walked to the front of the room where Helen sat at a table to the right of the podium with a small metal cash box, card file, and stack of cards in front of her. A dark-haired teenage girl sat beside her.

"Oh, hi," Helen said, smiling radiantly. "I'm so glad you came." She was so gracious that we expected a tray of canapes to appear at any moment. "Have you met my daughter?" she asked, introducing us.

We smiled and said hello. Now that we looked, there seemed to be a number of teenagers stacking books. "Are all of these yours?"

"No, just those two," she said, pointing to another girl and a boy. "The rest are their friends. They help out. It's really nice to have the kids here."

"We're thinking of bidding on something," we said.

"Oh," she said, smiling again. "I'm so glad. It's a lot of fun."

"Uh—how do we do it?"

"Oh, it's easy," she replied. "Just fill this out . . . ." She handed us a blank invoice form with a "46" on top and space to put our name, address, and dealer's resale number for sales tax exemption (we didn't have one of those). "Then you take this card . . ." It was a piece of construction paper about eight inches square with a "46" on it. "And hold it up every time you want to make a bid."

"Great. Thanks."

"You have a big advantage," she said, without bothering to lower her voice. "All the dealers have to mark up what they buy, so they never go higher than fifty percent of retail. Usually they try and get it for a third. You can top their bids and still get things for a lot less than you'd pay at a shop."

Armed with this information and clutching our little card, we moved back toward the folding chairs and tried to figure out where to sit. We decided on the second row because we wanted to make sure that Michael saw us when we raised our card to make a bid. As soon as we sat down, it was immediately apparent that our choice of seating was a tactical blunder. The savvier bidders had chosen to locate themselves in the rear in order to observe the competition without having to turn around.

Michael was at the lectern in the front now, waiting patiently as the remaining participants shuffled to their seats. No one seemed in much of a hurry.

"I'd like to begin if it is all right with you," Michael called, sounding a little annoyed and homey at the same time. The shuffling did not proceed any faster.

Finally, everyone was seated. It was six thirty-five. Lot 91 seemed a long way down the list and we wondered if we would be able to wait around until he got to it. Our baby-sitter had to leave by ten (Emily's ability to mimic language had progressed to the point that we were now using high school girls instead of Claire) and we had hoped to sneak in some dinner before we went home. Given the pace of other auctions we had observed—in *North by Northwest* for example—the likelihood of both bidding and eating began to seem remote.

Michael took his place. "Thank you all for coming," he began, sounding a bit like a traveling Shakespearean actor giving a reading in a Wild West saloon. "We will begin with lot number one." He held up an old, large book. *"A Complete Practical Treatise on Venereal Disease,"* he announced. "First edition, 1846. Contemporary boards, very worn, top board detached." He opened the book and held it high for all to see. There was a full-page picture of a man with hideous sores on his face. Michael paused. "With some remarkable chromolithographs," he added.

The auction proceeded at a surprisingly fast pace. It was rare that the bidding on any item exceeded ten seconds. No one bid on the venereal disease book at all. As soon as one book or group of books was auctioned, one or more of Michael's children or their friends picked up the books and carried them over to the winning bidder while the other kids paraded down the aisles with the next lot, opening the books so the audience could see them, then placing them on the table next to Michael for bids. Then, while the bidding on that item was being conducted, the kids would begin exhibiting the next.

The kids took their jobs very seriously. You could see the respect they had for their father, for the books, and for the process. An associate at Christie's handling a priceless Ming vase was no more serious and professional than these kids in T-shirts and baggy jeans walking up and down the aisles of the American Legion Hall in Sheffield. It was like watching a Frank Capra film.

All went well until about lot 20, when, while Michael was taking bids, there was a sudden *thud* in the left aisle. The boy who had dropped the book—he could not have been more than fifteen—just stood there, paralyzed, staring down at the floor with a look of horror on his face as though he had been baby-sitting and just dropped an infant. There was a momentary hesitation in the bidding but Michael never faltered. Except for a brief flick of his eyes in the direction of the incident, he continued the bidding as if dropping a book was a standard manner of exhibition.

In less than twenty minutes, we were halfway to lot 91. We

began to realize that the bidding went quickly because there was no hesitation, no agonizing over whether or not to go ten dollars higher. The dealers had obviously set strict limits on how much they would pay for any particular item (based on what they could sell it for, we supposed) and would not spend one penny more. Like the venereal disease book, many of the items were not bid on at all. Some went to bids that had been submitted in advance. In most cases, these bids were uncontested, as they seemed wildly higher than any of the dealers present were willing to pay.

Also, everyone here knew the rules. There was no "going once . . . going twice . . . third and last call . . . sold," the way they did it in the movies. This was rapid-fire. Michael would nod and vaguely point while he went:

"Tentwentythirtyfortyfiftysoldtonumbertwentyeight."

By and large, the estimated values in the catalogue were fair representations of the selling. Some went for less and a few, obscure items to us, went for a lot more. *Life on the Mississippi* sold for about $275.

Michael was on lot 89 when we realized that the kids were walking up and down the aisles with *our* set. They placed the ten Brontë books on the table next to the lectern. We leaned forward with clammy hands and fluttering hearts. Arnold Schwarzenegger bidding on John F. Kennedy's golf clubs did not feel any more tension than we did waiting to raise our little cardboard 46.

"Lot number ninety-one," announced Michael. *"The Novels of the Sisters Brontë.* Ten volumes. London, 1905. Original illustrations. Cloth. One or two covers a little worn or soiled. With six color plates by Dulac." He paused and held up one of the set. It was one of the clean ones. "Quite a charming little set," he noted. "We will start the bidding at thirty dollars."

We raised our 46 quickly.

"Thirtythirtyfivefortyfortyfive."

We thought he was sort of looking our way during parts of this process but we couldn't be sure so we just kept our card up.

"It's your bid," he finally said patiently, giving us the same look he'd given to the teenager who had dropped the book. "Sold to number forty-six," he said, with a little hint of a smile in the corner of his mouth, as one of the kids came up and solemnly handed us our ten books.

We sat for a little while longer after that, but we discovered we had no interest whatever in the proceedings once we had stopped bidding ourselves. We also realized that, once the dealers had bid on everything they wanted, they went up to the front and checked out. We still had time for a pizza, so we did, too.

When we got to the desk at the front, Helen was beaming.

We beamed right back. "We did it!"

"Congratulations," she said, taking out our invoice from the file. "You got a terrific deal."

She punched some numbers into a little pocket calculator, adding in the 10 percent buyer's premium and sales tax. "That will be fifty-one dollars and ninety-eight cents."

Sometime later, we ran into Michael at a book fair. We got to discussing his auction. The provocative ALS from Elizabeth Taylor came up.

"It was a letter to Harry Belafonte," Michael said.

"What was so provocative about it?"

"Oh. All it said was, 'Dear Harry. Fuck you.' "

"That was it?"

"That was it."

"Was 'fuck you' meant literally or figuratively?"

Michael shrugged. "You'd have to ask Liz," he said.

CHAPTER 11

Is this the place?"

"I think so. Let me check."

We were in New York. It was a clear, sunny, very warm Saturday afternoon and the streets were teeming in celebration of spring. Messengers hurtled along the streets and sidewalks, their bicycles weaving hysterically through crowds of weekend shoppers. Tourist groups, huddling close together for security while clutching their cameras, moved in phalanx from one building and store window to the next. The streets were locked in bumper-to-bumper traffic, taxis, buses, and trucks all jockeying frantically to try and finally make that next light. The air was filled with humidity and the sounds of horns, sirens, motors, and yelling and cursing in any number of languages. It was so noisy that the sounds blended together in one pounding din. It even *smelled* like New York.

We were on West Fifty-seventh Street, standing in front of number 30, an unassuming mid-rise building between Fifth and Sixth Avenues, the kind of place that in other sections of the city housed Korean import/export firms. In our hands were the little slips of paper on which we had written the names and addresses that we had found in the Antiquarian Booksellers Guide at the Pittsfield library. We looked up. On a picture window two stories above our heads, in two-foot-high letters it read: J. N. BARTFIELD FINE AND RARE BOOKS.

Up until this point, it had not been a particularly successful trip. We had already visited two other bookshops. The first was Ursus, which was located on the mezzanine floor of the Carlisle Hotel, on Madison Avenue and Seventy-seventh Street. Ursus was a very attractive shop, filled with old prints and finely bound books. The modern-first section was also nice, small but filled with a choice selection, Truman Capote, Graham Greene, Hemingway, and others, all in excellent condition, some inscribed.

Next to the first-edition section were two desks, each occupied by a slim and extremely pretty young woman with fashionably cut blond hair, dressed in an understated and tasteful print dress. Neither was overly accessorized nor overly made up. They looked as if they had walked into Ursus immediately upon receiving their undergraduate degrees in English literature from Smith or Wellesley. The young woman on the left seemed absorbed in paperwork. When we walked in, she looked up and asked in a perfunctory manner if she could help us. When we replied that we just wanted to browse, she turned away sharply and made it a point to offer no further assistance. The young woman on the right was on the telephone.

"Oh yes, Dr. W——," she was saying, in a respectful and cultured voice, "I am well aware of that. That's why I'm calling. When we saw that it was not in the condition we had been led to expect, we thought to inform you immediately . . . Oh no, of course not. You have no further obligation. We assume full responsibility . . . Oh yes, of course we will continue to seek a copy in the condition you require. It is no trouble at all, I assure you. That is what we're here for . . . Absolutely. We'll keep you informed of our progress . . . Oh, you're quite welcome, Dr. W——."

She hung up and spun around in her chair so that she could face the young woman on the left and, coincidentally, us.

"That man is such a *prick,*" she said.

Our next stop had been Argosy on Fifty-ninth Street. Argosy is a large, multistory used-book store, one of the best known in New York, and we had been intending to go for some time.

When we walked in, we stopped at a desk in the front and checked our backpacks. To our right, along the front wall, were shelves of old leatherbound books on the most esoteric of subjects, like the 1847 town records of Beekman, New York. These books were marked "$25 each." We opened one and the inside was a mess. There was water damage and missing pages.

The first floor was about one hundred feet deep and, for most of its length, about thirty feet wide. The shelves and bookcases against the walls were old, dark wood and the lighting fixtures, also seemingly from another, more genteel time, hung down from a high ceiling.

The first thing we did was walk through to the back and go downstairs to the basement where the preponderance of used books were kept. It was stifling hot and it was immediately clear that if there was something worth having, it was not going to be worth looking for. There were thousands of used books down there, most in the ten- to twenty-dollar range, but they could charitably be described as in poor condition.

Almost immediately, we returned to the main floor, where Argosy had its "recommended" section of used books. The stock here was in much better condition and the selection was more manageable but the prices seemed extraordinarily high for what they were selling. For example, the three-volume Heritage Press edition of Boswell's *Life of Johnson,* an excellent set of which we had purchased at Berkshire Book Company for thirty-five dollars, was here selling for a hundred and it was in far worse shape. Books that we had regularly seen at any number of used-book stores for ten and fifteen dollars, were here at thirty-five and fifty dollars.

We were just about to leave when we spotted a sign for Argosy's old-and-rare-book section at a cluttered desk in the middle of the room. That might be interesting, we thought. There wasn't anybody at the desk, so we approached the woman behind the checkout counter at the front of the store.

"We'd like to see the rare-book section, please."

"I'm sorry. That section is closed. Mrs. Lowry who manages our rare books isn't in on Saturday," she said. "Just Mondays through Fridays. Please stop back then."

We looked around. The store was not particularly crowded and there were three or four employees who seemed not to be doing much of anything.

"Couldn't someone else let us in? We've come from out of town and we won't be here on Monday."

"I'm afraid not. It's locked." She paused. "But let me give you one of Mrs. Lowry's cards. Maybe you can call the next time you're in New York."

Now we stood in front of the building that housed J. N. Bartfield's Fine and Rare Books and wondered if this, too, would be a disappointment. Perhaps they didn't work on Saturdays, either. But we were already there, so we went ahead and opened the heavy metal and smoked-glass front door and walked inside.

As soon as the door closed behind us, the noise from the street (as well as most of the light) disappeared, and we found ourselves in a cool, hushed, darkened hall. There was a directory on the wall to our right and a desk at the end of the hall that was obviously meant for a security guard although no one was in sight.

"J. N. Bartfield Fine and Rare Books," we confirmed on the directory. "Third floor."

The hall was L-shaped and the building's one elevator was in the short leg, an alcove to the left of the security desk. Once we turned the corner, all remaining signs of the street disappeared.

The elevator was on seven, the top floor. We pushed the button and waited. For several minutes nothing happened. Then the elevator started to descend. It went to six and seemed to stop. Then to five . . . four . . . three . . . two. The light stayed on so long at each floor we assumed that, despite the deserted lobby, many people were getting on and off at each stop. Several times we were tempted to walk, but the doorway to the stairs was covered with a locked metal grille.

Finally, the elevator got to the ground floor and the doors began to creak open. We stepped back to let all the people out but there was no one there. The elevator was empty. We looked at each other, got in, and pushed the button for the third floor. After a long time, the doors closed and the elevator ascended—slowly, slowly—to the third floor. Once again, the elevator door creaked open and we stepped out. As soon as we did, the door closed quickly behind us.

There was a plate glass door on either side of the hall. The one on the left read J. N. BARTFIELD FINE ART. We looked through the glass and saw several large paintings of cowboys and buffaloes, but otherwise, the gallery, like the elevator and the hallway, was deserted. The plate-glass door on the right read J. N. BARTFIELD FINE AND RARE BOOKS. We looked inside. There was no sign of life there, either.

We tried the handle of the door to the bookshop, but the door was locked. A sign read PLEASE BUZZ FOR ENTRY. After a moment's hesitation, we buzzed. We waited. Finally, there was an answering buzz. We turned the door handle and walked in.

The room we entered was rectangular, about twenty by thirty feet, as hushed and still as the rest of the building. There were no windows, no classical music piped in from concealed speakers, no murmur of conversation coming from some unseen corner of the shop. The room was perfectly climate controlled but there was no hum of air-conditioning. Everything was still, with no sight or sound of the outside world.

The room itself was magnificent. The walls consisted of floor-to-ceiling bookcases made of highly polished mahogany or cherry that shone in the artificial light emanating from recesses in the ceiling. On the shelves were the rich browns, blues, greens, and reds of the books, the leather gleaming softly, luxurious and discreet. Some of the covers had amazingly intricate filigree designs worked into the spine.

The bookcases on the left and right stopped short of the far wall, apparently leading to other sections of the shop. A massive, ornate rectangular claw-foot oak table sat square in the center of the room on a polished hardwood floor. There were no chairs.

Then, suddenly, two men emerged from the opening at the right.

The first was stooped and balding. He wore glasses and looked to be about seventy years old. He was shuffling along, squinting sourly over the tops of his glasses, peering at us from either side of a prominent nose. He was dressed in a black sweatsuit, a neck warmer, and mustard-colored shoes, Ebenezer Scrooge in leisure wear.

Half a step behind him was a very handsome, unsmiling man of about thirty, pale, slender, and artistic looking, dressed in a light gray polo shirt, buttoned to the top, no tie, with a soft light brown suit and brown lace-ups. Here was Bob Cratchit, just returned from Barney's.

The older man stopped and frowned at us. "How did you find us?" he demanded, without bothering with pleasantries. "We control our advertising very carefully."

"Uh . . ." Despite all that had gone before, we were unprepared for this greeting. Was this a trick question? After all, the man had two-foot-high letters on his front window. There was also a prominent advertisement for J. N. Bartfield Fine and Rare Books in the Yellow Pages. "We went to the library and checked in the *Antiquarian Bookseller's Guide*," we replied.

This was apparently an unsatisfactory answer. The man in the sweatsuit abruptly turned away and headed back from whence he had just emerged. "Well, perhaps Kevin can help you," he said, not bothering to turn and look at us. "Kev-in!" he barked, just before disappearing around the corner.

The younger man, who was still no more than two feet away from us, stepped forward. This, it seemed, was Kevin.

"We'd just like to look around, if that's all right," we said, speaking very softly in the quiet of the room.

"Of course," said Kevin, equally softly, stepping back. He was very polite but the words came out stiffly, as if he had memorized lines for a play and didn't quite have them down yet.

We walked to the wall opposite the door and began to browse. The books were all in sets. Shakespeare, Swift, Molière, Voltaire, Goethe, Dante, Schiller, Aristotle, Plato, one beautiful set after another, sometimes two or three or four different sets of the same author.

"Are you looking for anything in particular?" asked Kevin, padding soundlessly behind us.

"Dickens?"

"Dickens is over here," said Kevin.

J. N. Bartfield's had three sets of Dickens, a blue one, a green one, and a red one. Each contained over twenty volumes. We removed the first volume of the red set. It was *The Pickwick Papers*. We opened the cover. It contained the original title page, text, and illustrations. You didn't need *ABC for Book-Collectors* in J. N. Bartfield's. There wasn't any foxing, or sunning; nothing was chipped, torn, bubbled, shaken, or rubbed. Although this set had been printed in the 1870s, the pages were as crisp and unsoiled as if the book had spent the last 120 years in a climate-controlled vault.

We turned to the free endpaper, which is the blank page opposite the front cover where dealers customarily enter the price in pencil. There was nothing. We put back *The Pickwick Papers* and took out *Oliver Twist*. There was no price there either.

"We keep the first book of each set over here," said Kevin, gesturing to a bookcase on the right. "You'll find the price of the set inside the front cover."

We followed him to the bookcase where the first volumes were kept. Smoothly but delicately, Kevin withdrew a red volume, *Sketches by "Boz,"* from a middle shelf. He opened the cover and there, written in pencil, was a little number.

"This set is twelve thousand dollars," he said.

Kevin must have noticed a slight change in our expressions because he reached for the first volume of the green Dickens. "We have another set that is less expensive," he said, opening that *Sketches by "Boz."* His voice had no echo, no residue, like a man standing in the sun and casting no shadow. "This one is ninety-five hundred dollars but it is not nearly as well done as the other. One volume of this set, I think it's *David Copperfield,* has been rebound. It was done professionally, of course, but still, any rebinding detracts from the value." Then he handed each of us one of the books. They seemed to come our way at not quite full speed. "Also, if you'll notice, the gilt work on the binding is not as intricate and the illustrations in the less expensive set are not as clearly rendered as those in the more expensive set."

We looked at both volumes. The illustrations in the red set had a bit more contrast but it wasn't like the illustrations in the green set were smudged or something.

We handed back the books and glanced around. We noticed *Sense and Sensibility* on a higher shelf.

"Jane Austen?"

Kevin removed a deep blue volume from the shelf. "Yes," he said. "This is a six-volume 1892 edition, published by Little, Brown and Company." He turned the book so that we could see the spine and the cover. "As you can see," he said, "the spine is slightly faded. That is true of the entire set, although the fading is even."

The spine *was* slightly faded. These books actually had a flaw. "How much is this?" we asked. Our curiosity as to the price of the set certainly did not spring from any intention of buying it. This was our first detailed exposure to "fine and rare books" that were not first editions. It was like wondering what a Fabergé egg would cost.

"I believe it is twenty-one hundred dollars." He opened the front cover to check. "Yes."

"Really."

He returned Jane Austen to her place. For a moment, the three of us stood there. We didn't want to leave. It was intoxicating being in Bartfield's, in the cool and the quiet, where everything moved slowly, surrounded by magnificent works of art. But more than that, for as long as we were there, we could pretend that we belonged there. All the same, we were impostors. Kevin was treating us like customers when we knew we weren't. We would have loved to have been, but we weren't. If Kevin had made the slightest dismissive move or gesture, we would have been gone in a second.

But instead he asked, "Is there anything else you'd like to see?"

We looked at him, trying to decide if the question was perfunctory or, worse, sarcastic. But there was no sign of that. He seemed genuine.

"Do you have anything that isn't in a set?"

"Yes," he replied. "We have some individual volumes and small sets in the other room."

He directed us toward the opening to the left of the front door. We now saw that the sidewalls were actually floor-to-ceiling partitions and Kevin was leading us to a closed door set back about ten feet into the opening. The door was locked. He took a key out of his pocket and opened it.

It led to another room, a smaller version of the first and, if anything, even quieter. It was about fifteen feet square but completely ringed by bookcases, making it feel even more intimate. Suddenly, the books were very close to us.

"Literature is over here," Kevin said, pointing to a section two steps away.

We walked over and immediately found ourselves face-to-face with *Bleak House*.

Bleak House is a great book. It is considered by many to be Dickens's masterpiece, one of the greatest novels ever written in the English language. Although, on its face, *Bleak House* is a satiric indictment of the British court system, Dickens's brush is much broader than that. *Bleak House* is about the mistreatment of children, the hypocrisy of the upper classes, false charity, and vain hopes. It is filled with mystery, satire, suspense, pathos, and intrigue.

Charles Dickens was a court reporter in his youth and a prodigious stenographer. But, more than that, nearly every day of his working career he stopped writing at 2:30 in the afternoon to walk the streets of London, sometimes twenty to thirty miles at a time. When he was working hard he would sometimes walk all night, complaining that his characters were pulling at his coattails. He walked in the slums and he walked in Hyde Park and he walked into taverns and shops and inns. As a result, his portraits, while often hilarious, are timeless and chillingly real. And nowhere is this talent for characterization more evident than in *Bleak House*. Not a day goes by that someone or other doesn't remind us of Harold Skimpole or Mrs. Jellyby.

This *Bleak House* was in two volumes, bound in dark blue leather. We took out the first and began to leaf through it.

"That was part of a set that someone broke up," said Kevin, "although I can't imagine why anyone would. It's an 1874 edition, bound by Zaehnsdorf, with all the original illustrations. If the set was complete, it would easily be the most expensive in the shop."

Looking over the shelves, we now saw, in various places, a similarly bound, two-volume *Our Mutual Friend,* single volumes for *Great Expectations* and *Hard Times,* as well as a number of others. We opened the cover of Volume I of *Bleak House*. A little notation in pencil read "350×."

"This is only three hundred fifty dollars?" we asked. We never would have thought to apply the word "only" to $350 before.

"No," said Kevin. He pointed at the "×." "This means that the price is three hundred fifty dollars for each volume."

"Oh."

"I'm afraid that's the way we notate our books," he said.

"Seven hundred, huh?"

"I'm afraid so."

We put *Bleak House* back. It was on a middle shelf right next to us, perfectly placed so that we could see it every time we turned our heads.

Kevin didn't change expression a whole lot or alter the tone of his voice but somehow, in this little room, he seemed happier. "I have some other things you might enjoy looking at," he said.

"Sure."

He opened the door to one of the cabinets that made up the bottom section of the bookcases and withdrew a three-volume set, each in a black leather slipcase, and put them on the table. "This is very unusual," Kevin said. "Take a look."

We withdrew the first volume from the slipcase. There was an exquisite painting, like a cameo, set into the front cover.

"It's Napoléon's memoirs in an exhibition binding done by Riviere in 1885," said Kevin. "Each volume has a hand-painted ivory miniature mounted on the front and back. On the front is a portrait of Napoléon at a different stage of his life and on the backs are Josephine, Marie Louise, and the King of Rome. It's wonderfully illustrated. And look at the gilt work. It's marvelous, isn't it?"

"Yes," we said, feeling the leather on the front and looking at the miniature. "How much does something like this sell for?"

"Ninety-five hundred dollars," he said. "Wait. Here's something else. These are wonderful." Leaving Napoléon's memoirs on the table, Kevin opened the door to another of the cabinets and withdrew two volumes in a light brown binding that we recognized from Clarence's Shakespeare set as Nonesuch Press.

"This is Homer in the original Greek with Pope's translation," Kevin said, opening one of the volumes. "You can see," he continued, "on the left is the Greek, on the facing page, the translation. It's Nonesuch Press, printed in 1931. They only printed thirteen hundred of the *Odyssey* and thirteen hundred fifty of the *Iliad*. You can't polish them, so there are very few left. The set is fifteen hundred dollars."

"Can't polish them?"

"Yes. Most binders use calf or morocco . . . morocco is goatskin, small 'm' . . . you can use British Museum formula to keep the bindings from deteriorating . . ."

"British Museum formula?"

"It's a special polish that keeps the leather shiny and supple. You have to know how to use it but if you bring your books to a professional every ten years or so . . . more often if you live in a humid climate or near the ocean . . . the bindings can stay in perfect condition almost indefinitely. But Nonesuch Press used salmon niger morocco, which discolors when it's polished. Over time, Nonesuch Press editions are going to get more and more rare."

We leafed through the Homer.

"Here," Kevin continued while we were still examining

Homer, this time removing a volume from a middle shelf on the wall near the door. "Look at this." He handed us a book, *Four Months in Algeria; with a visit to Carthage,* by Joseph William Blakesley, published in 1859. While it was nicely bound in red leather, it was not in nearly as good condition as his previous offerings and the subject, while interesting, seemed obscure. We looked it over briefly and made to hand it back.

"Take a closer look," he said. "See if you can figure out why this book is special."

We turned the book over to look at it from every angle. We opened the book and leafed through it. "Is it the illustrations?" we asked. There were a number of color plates and fold-out maps, although nothing that seemed unique.

"Not in there," said Kevin.

We closed the book and looked on the outside but there were no other illustrations to be seen.

Kevin took back the book. "Watch," he said, then opened the front cover and held the pages at an angle so that just the end of each page was visible, like a deck of cards fanned out on a table top.

A painting appeared, ships in a harbor with hills in the background. The colors were rich and the detail fabulous.

"This is called fore-edge painting," said Kevin. "It was originally done in Italy in the fifteenth and sixteenth centuries but was most popular in England in the eighteenth and nineteenth centuries."

"How do they do it?"

"The artist has a press that holds the pages in the correct position while he paints. He has to work relatively quickly so that the pages don't stay in that position too long and become damaged. When the paint is dry, the book is closed and the edges are gilded in the normal way." Then he let the pages fall back to their natural position and the painting disappeared. "If they are not aware of it, a person can own a book with a fore-edge painting for years and never know that they own something special." He fanned the pages again and the painting reappeared.

"Is that how you get them?"

"Sometimes. We don't see that many. Usually fore-edge painted books have been bought by collectors long before they get to us."

We nodded. It was amazing, being so close—touching books like these, which we could never hope to own, of whose existence we hadn't even been aware. Books with ivory miniatures on the front and paintings on the side. It was like getting a private showing in the Louvre.

"If you like Dickens," said Kevin quietly, even for him, "I've got a treat for you."

He opened the door to one of the cabinets and withdrew a red box big enough to hold a hefty-size volume. He placed it flat on the table with the spine of the box facing him so that we could not see what it was.

"We just got this," he said. "It's very special." He proceeded to open the box, which folded open, and took out the contents, five red sleeves, and placed them on the table. Then, gently, almost tenderly, he lifted the first of the series, a thin book, bound in red leather, out of its sleeve. We still had no idea what it was.

Kevin placed his hand on the cover. "This is a first edition, first state. There were only six thousand printed and very few are left. I've never heard of one in this fine a condition before." Then, he lifted his hand and opened the cover to the title page.

"A Christmas Carol. In Prose," it read. *"Being a Ghost Story of Christmas.* By Charles Dickens. Chapman & Hall, Publishers, 1843. John Leech, Illustrator."

"Dickens supervised the entire printing himself," said Kevin, incredibly handing us this book. "He wanted everything to be just so, and to use red and green, which was very expensive. In fact, the green endpapers are one of the main bibliographic points of the first issue. Also, four of the illustrations are in color. Find one, they're wonderful."

Very, very slowly and very, very carefully we turned the pages until we found a color illustration of Fezzywig dancing at his Christmas party. For all we knew, Charles Dickens himself had touched this book.

And now, so had we.

After another moment or two, we gave *A Christmas Carol* back to Kevin. Then, as if someone had called our name, we both turned to the right. *Bleak House* had not moved. It was still on the shelf, looking at us.

When we turned back, Kevin had replaced *A Christmas Carol* in its sleeve and was putting it back in the box.

"How long have you been here?" we asked.

"Not too long," he replied. "Just over a year. I worked in another bookstore before this, but the books here are beautiful."

"And that's J. N. Bartfield? The other man when we came in?"

"No," Kevin replied. "J. N. Bartfield was his brother. That's Mr. Murray."

We thought that we had heard wrong or Kevin had meant to say just "Murray." "How long has he been doing this?" we asked.

"He's been here for thirty-seven years," Kevin replied. "Before that, he and his brother ran the rare-book department at Brentano's when Brentano's had a real rare-book department. In fact, we still have some books that are stamped 'Brentano's.' He knows more about rare books and fine bindings than anyone I've ever spoken to."

"Who buys these books?" we asked. "Collectors?"

"Sometimes," Kevin replied. "But most of our clients are interested in amassing a library."

It was time to go. "Thank you," we said. Anything else seemed inadequate. We turned to look at *Bleak House* one last time.

"You know, if you're really interested in that, Mr. Murray might be willing to discount it a bit since the set is already broken."

Bleak House was off the shelf and in our hands before he had finished the sentence.

"How much?"

"I'm not sure, but he might be willing to give it to you for six hundred."

In this small, sealed corner of the universe, surrounded by first edition *Christmas Carols* and ten-thousand-dollar books with hand-painted miniatures of Napoléon, six hundred seemed like a deal.

"All right," we said.

"No, I can't do that," said Mr. Murray, shaking his head, frowning, and leaning over the table in the main room, peering over the top of his glasses. "Let me show you what you're paying for. Here. This is a Zaehnsdorf binding." He pointed to little red flowers on the spine. "These are hand-painted floral onlays set into the spine. Excellent condition. Very unusual."

A hundred dollars for some little red flowers? We hadn't even noticed the little red flowers. We looked down at Mr. Murray, then glanced quickly at Kevin who, still without changing expression, was looking embarrassed.

"Okay," we said. "We'll take it anyway."

Mr. Murray softened. "Leave it with us. We'll polish it and mail it to you. You'll save the tax."

Within moments, we were back out on Fifty-seventh Street. It was hot, humid, crowded, and noisy.

"Holy shit! We just spent seven hundred dollars!"

CHAPTER 12

*B*leak House was delivered by UPS a week later. It came in a box at least three times the size of the books themselves. The box was made of thick cardboard, within which were two layers of bubble wrap, newspaper, brown wrapping paper, white tissue paper, and, finally, the books.

We unwrapped all the layers. The two volumes shone. (We assumed they had been polished, although they were so beautiful it was hard to tell.) We put them in our best bookcase in the center of an eye-level shelf that had been specially cleared for their arrival. We then spent the next two weeks stopping at that bookcase, looking at the books, removing the books, delicately leafing through the pages to look at the illustrations, running our fingers over the bindings, and staring reverently at our incredibly expensive little red florets.

It was only after we had cooed nauseatingly over *Bleak House* for those two weeks that we realized that there were rare book dealers right in the Berkshires who might have things we'd like to see.

Immediately upon that revelation, we returned to our trusty Yellow Pages to check out the listings for the very dealers we had previously avoided. The closest seemed to be John R. Sanderson Rare Books in Stockbridge, the town immediately south of Lenox.

The listing gave the address as West Main Street, which we found a little puzzling. We knew Stockbridge intimately (not a particularly tall order) and could not remember seeing anything that resembled a bookshop, let alone a rare-book shop, on Main Street. We called to confirm the address and a soft-spoken man assured us that the listing was correct and told us where to find his shop. We arranged to visit in the early afternoon of the same day.

We followed the instructions and ended up in front of a modest, two-story, milk chocolate brown house with dark chocolate brown shutters, about one hundred yards west of the historic Red Lion Inn, the sprawling, world-famous hostelry where tourists come and pay exorbitant prices for gelatinous chicken pot pie and overcooked Yankee pot roast. It was an old house, as were the others on the street, and it had a little garden in front with those huge hostas that Realtors always extol as "mature perennials." There was no sign, nothing on the door, no indication whatever that this was anything other than someone's home.

Hoping we were not about to disturb some flinty, privacy-loving New Englander who greeted strangers with a shotgun or a large dog, we rang the buzzer and waited. Within seconds, the door was opened by a tall, thin man in his middle forties with light brown hair and a wispy mustache wearing a golf shirt.

"Hello," he said. "I'm John Sanderson. I apologize for making the appointment so late, but I just got back." There was a set of golf clubs leaning against the wall behind him. "Did you find the place all right?"

"Oh, yes. The directions were perfect."

"Good," he said, smiling briefly.

Even in person, John Sanderson's voice had a slightly muffled, whisperlike quality, as if, when he was a child, he had been taught repeatedly never to raise it. And although he had no accent, there was a vaguely English quality about him. He was scholarly, the sort of person you'd expect to find in a carrel at the British Museum, poring over primary reference materials for an exhaustive biography of Chaucer.

The front door opened up into a small entranceway. We walked in and shook hands all around. There was a dining room to the right and a living room to the left but the furnishings seemed to predate a man of John Sanderson's age. A small table stood just to the side, adorned with little stacks of flyers for future book fairs and rosters of the area's antiquarian book dealers.

"This way," he said, turning toward a door set in the wall under the staircase that went up to the second floor. He opened the door to reveal a steep, narrow, carpeted staircase that led into the basement.

We realized why we had never noticed an antiquarian bookshop on West Main Street before. Unlike David and Esther or "Books Bruce & Sue Gventer," John Sanderson didn't run his business *near* his house. He ran his business *in* his house. John R. Sanderson Rare Books was apparently located in John R. Sanderson's basement. Being in somebody's basement to look at books was a new experience and a little disquieting. We didn't know whether to act like customers, guests, or the exterminator.

Nonetheless, we followed him down, single file, to the bottom of the stairs that ended within about a foot of the back wall of the house and effectively bisected the basement. To the right was a room filled with piles of cardboard boxes, behind which was a set of floor-to-ceiling metal shelves with large reference-looking books on them. There was another golf bag leaning against the wall, just inside the door.

To the left was a room about fifteen feet square that was packed with glass-fronted bookcases, handmade bookcases, built-in bookcases, oak bookcases, pine bookcases, mahogany bookcases, and all other varieties of bookcases, each of which had every free inch filled with books. There must have been two thousand books in the room, maybe more. The aisles, what there were of them, were impossibly narrow, narrower than the stairway, and that took some doing.

The only space on the wall that was not covered with books contained a single window that looked out on John Sanderson's backyard. John Sanderson's backyard happened to be the eighteenth tee of the Stockbridge Golf Club. You could see the golf carts tooling around and people in green pants hitting balls onto the fairway.

"You keep the books in your basement?" we couldn't help asking.

"Actually, this used to be part of the kitchen," said John. "This was a dumbwaiter," he added, pointing at a narrow case now filled to the ceiling with books. "Food used to be made down here and sent up."

"And that's the golf club? Don't you worry that people will hit their golf balls through the windows?"

"It's a risk but I like the convenience," he said.

"You play a lot?" In a shop, we would have headed right for the books. But here, in someone's home, it seemed only polite to make a bit of conversation first.

"Eight handicap," he said. "Maybe a seven. I used to be a five." He paused. "I shot a sixty-seven the other day, and that's good on this course."

"Ah." Polite conversation thus exhausted, we turned our attention to the books.

"Are you interested in anything in particular?" he asked.

The dreaded question. "We'd just like to look around, if we could."

"Certainly. Twentieth-century fiction is here, at the near wall, nineteenth- and twentieth-century American and English literature is over there, New England and Americana are here," he said, indicating some shelves in the middle, "and there are also books on navigation, birds, agriculture, books before 1800 . . ."

He stood in the doorway and watched while we browsed.

We started with his twentieth-century literature section that was to our immediate left. It consisted of two six-foot-high, knocked-together pine-board bookcases. The selection was odd. It didn't seem to reflect any particular taste or focus. A lot of the books were the first English editions of American writers. *The Mansion* was there, by Faulkner, a substantial number of books by Jack London, a couple of books by Hemingway, including *A Farewell to Arms,* Max Beerbohm, Truman Capote, Norman Mailer, Nelson Algren, and Daphne du Maurier intermixed with books like *Clockers* by Richard Price.

We opened the covers and peeked at the prices. Most of the books were in the $100 to $250 range. We were surprised. We had seen a number of these books elsewhere for a good deal more. *The Mansion,* for example, a flawless copy of which John Sanderson was selling for sixty-five dollars, we had seen at a book fair for well over a hundred. He had both a first American edition and a first English edition of Jack London's *Sea Wolf.* We were unfamiliar with the English edition, but we knew that the first American edition, even without a dust jacket, could sell for between four and five hundred dollars. Here it was $175.

Hmmm.

"Where do you get your books?" we asked.

"Oh, here and there," John replied. "I go to London every year."

That explained all the English firsts.

"Are you English?"

"No, but I did my graduate work there."

"In what?"

He gave a little smile. "I got my Ph.D. in Elizabethan drama," he said. "I wrote my dissertation on the second part of two part plays in Elizabethan and Jacobean drama. You know, sequels. I was interested in the relationship of the second part to the first part."

Chaucer hadn't been such a bad guess after all. "What did you come up with?"

"Oh, nothing of great interest," he said. "Academic stuff mostly."

"Is that how you became a book dealer?"

"Well, in a roundabout way, I suppose. I finished in 1975 and came back here. There weren't too many teaching jobs. I had an academic library of my own and I had read many old books on microfilm and was conscious of their importance. So when I got back here I started buying books."

We nodded and continued to move through the room. The basement was divided into categories, the same categories you might expect to find at a Barnes and Noble—travel, psychology, history, fantasy, and science fiction—but the books in those categories were slightly different than those in a modern bookstore. For one thing, most of them were finely bound, many with gilt or raised bands, and all were old, the preponderance from the eighteenth and nineteenth centuries. They weren't in the condition of the books at Bartfield's. Many of the spines were rubbed and we saw some cracked hinges as well as a good deal of foxing. But on the whole, for books of this age, they were in good condition.

But it was the titles that really set this stock apart. John Sanderson's basement was a little book fair unto itself. A representative sampling of the books he had for sale were:

A Botanist in the Amazon Valley,
Deer Forests of Scotland,
Snuff and Snuff Boxes,
Games and Sports in the Army,
Omens and Superstitions of Southern India,
The Pipe Book,
A Study of British Genius,
The Insane in the United States and Canada,

and, finally,

Possession: Demoniacal and Other.

"Do you really sell these?" we asked.

"Oh, yes. There are people around who collect almost everything."

"Who would you sell this to, for example?" we asked, pointing at *Possession: Demoniacal and Other.*

He shrugged. "Maybe a rich psychoanalyst."

Moving on from exotica, we went to the nineteenth-century-fiction section at the back of the cellar. This area occupied most of another pine-board bookcase, about six feet high by about eight feet wide. There were a good number of unusual titles here as well, things like *The Gypsies and the Detectives* and *Strikers, Communists, Tramps and Detectives* by Allan Pinkerton, but also an excellent selection of more serious literature, choice and just to our taste. Hawthorne, Emerson, Twain, James Russell Lowell, Walt Whitman, Stephen Crane, Ambrose Bierce, Poe, W. Dean Howells, and Henry James. All the books were firsts or notable for some other reason. Here again, most of the books were in good but not great condition. None looked like they had been stored in a vault. John Sanderson obviously bought books that people had read.

When we checked the prices, we saw that once again, for the good stuff, most of the books were in the $150 to $350 range, but also once again, these were far lower than prices for comparable books that we had seen elsewhere.

There were three or four Henry James novels that were especially tempting. James is difficult, dense, minutely concerned with the nuances of social interaction, and completely wonderful. During a long and productive career in which he produced twenty-two novels, over one hundred "tales," the equivalent of about ten books of literary criticism as well as biography and reams of notable letters, James exerted enormous influence on such other writers as Joseph Conrad, Edith Wharton, James Joyce, Virginia Woolf, William Faulkner, and Graham Greene.

A first edition of one of James's better-known works could only become more expensive with time because, despite his literary reputation, he was never a commercial success and consequently, unlike his contemporary and friend Edith Wharton who routinely wrote best-sellers, he never had a large first printing. In fact, after Edith Wharton published *The House of Mirth,* she wrote a letter to James in which she mentioned that, with the proceeds of her last novel, she had bought a motorcar and intended to bring it with her to Europe in order to take him driving. James replied in his letter that, with the proceeds of *his* last novel he had purchased a wheelbarrow, and with the proceeds of his next, he hoped to have it painted.

Now, staring us in the face, were two copies of *The Awkward Age,* one for $150 and the other for $200. They were both first American editions, first issue, two of only a thousand copies printed. Neither had a dust jacket, although who knew if *The Awkward Age* had even been issued with one? The spine on the $150 copy was slightly cracked and severely rubbed at the top and there was some foxing inside. The pages of the $200 copy, on the other hand, were only a little bit soiled and the cover was virtually flawless. We knew enough by now to immediately put the cheaper copy back.

We leafed through the more expensive one once again. Two hundred dollars. A lot of money (even for our post–*Bleak House* period), but it seemed remarkably inexpensive considering the scant number of copies that had been printed. And, if we were correct, this book might be two or three times as expensive the next time we considered buying it. But we didn't know for sure, so we put it down as a "maybe" and moved on.

We had almost come full circle when John said, "Did you see the Edith Whartons?"

"No." We began to turn back to the shelves.

"No, no," he said. "I keep them over here. There's a lot of local interest."

Right next to the staircase stood a small cart with a pile of about ten books on it.

"They're not all first editions," John said.

We started to go through them. About the third book down was a red, three-quarter morocco, beautifully bound copy of *The Custom of the Country.* We opened the cover. "$160."

"That one is a first," said John Sanderson.

Now Edith Wharton was also a terrific writer. Not quite in Henry James's league (in our opinion) but, as we mentioned, much more popular. And, just at that time, Edith Wharton was hot, as hot as a turn-of-the-century writer was going to get. Her posthumous novel, *The Buccaneers,* had just been republished and PBS was doing a miniseries based on it, lavishly filmed in Newport. Martin Scorsese had recently put out *The Age of Innocence* with Daniel Day-Lewis and Michelle Pfeiffer. People were *reading* Edith Wharton again. She was the current number one in the cultural writer of the month club. (Thanks to Emma Thompson, she has been subsequently supplanted by Jane Austen.)

Moreover, she was a Berkshire writer. Her books were all over the county but much harder to find elsewhere in the country. We *knew* that $160 for a first edition of *The Custom of the Country,* even rebacked, was a good deal. We might have suspected, even strongly suspected, that the Henry James was a good deal, too, but this we *knew* was a good deal. And the book itself was so beautifully bound, so really exquisite . . .

"I'll be happy to take a check," John said helpfully.

Next up was Howard S. Mott, Rare Books and Autographs. Howard S. Mott, Rare Books and Autographs, or, as they were known to almost everyone we spoke to, "The Motts," conducted their business out of an imposing yellow and white colonial that sat behind tall hedges on Route 7 in Sheffield, just north of Berkshire Book Company.

Our knowledge of the Motts was extremely limited, gleaned from bits of conversation dropped by other local dealers, none of it encouraging: The Motts were "old-line dealers"; the father, Howard, now in his late eighties, had been in the book business for almost sixty years; his son, Donald, known as "Rusty," ran most of the day-to-day affairs; they dealt in Americana; everything they owned was extremely expensive; you *must* have an appointment to get in to see the books; you could only get an appointment if they decided you were worth it; they often didn't keep their appointments; if they did keep their appointment but they didn't like you once you got there, they would throw you out; if they didn't throw you out and you wanted to buy something, they thought nothing of raising the price penciled in a book while you were standing there.

Consequently, there had been some discussion in our home as to just who it would be that made the telephone call requesting the appointment.

"Hello? Is this the Motts?"

"Yes," replied a man's voice.

So far so good.

"My name is Nancy Goldstone. I wonder if my husband, Larry, and I could see your books?"

"Are you a dealer?"

"No."

"What are you interested in?"

"Americana."

"Certainly. When would you like to come over?"

This was the first time we ever "dressed" to go to look at books. We got in the car, drove to Sheffield, turned into the driveway marked HOWARD S. MOTT, RARE BOOKS AND AUTOGRAPHS, and pulled in right behind a plumber's truck. We got out of the car, stepped up to the front door, and rang the bell. We felt like the kids who had gone to the one house on the street that everyone had warned us to stay away from on Halloween.

After a few minutes, the door was opened by a tall, large, red-haired man, balding at the top, who appeared to be in his early forties. He was wearing a short-sleeve button-down shirt open at the collar with a pair of walking shorts. There was an about six-inch-long tattoo of an anchor on his left forearm that did not appear to have been done recently. The son, we thought cleverly.

"Are you the Goldstones?" he asked. He seemed a little shy, but not at all unfriendly.

"Yes."

"Hi. I'm Rusty Mott. Won't you come in?"

We stepped inside. There were high ceilings and a stairway leading up from the entranceway to the second floor. Some tables with small stacks of what appeared to be catalogues stood against the wall to the right but otherwise it just looked like an elderly person's home.

The furnishings were sort of shabbily genteel, the Oriental rugs worn, the walls needed paint. There was a track next to the wall on the stair-case to accommodate a special chair to take someone up and down.

"You said you were interested in Americana?" said Rusty.

"Uh, yes. We like literature, too." Modern firsts was clearly out of the question. This was not a modern firsts sort of house.

"Well, why don't you start in here," he said, gesturing to a room off the hall on the left. He led us inside. It was another high-ceilinged room, a parlor with chairs and sofas and lamps on the tables and a fireplace with a grate in front. It was almost entirely ringed by floor-to-ceiling bookcases. There were three or four stools placed at in-tervals around the room so people could examine the top shelves. In the center of the front wall was a large, what appeared to be colonial painting of a fleshy, exceptionally unattractive man in a wig with puffy lips and a Nixonian five o'clock shadow.

"I think it's British," said Rusty, while we examined the paint-ing, "but my friends tell me it's American, like Peter Pelham doing John Cotton. I hope it's Peter Pelham because then it's worth a lot of money." Then he indicated the books on the shelves. "We keep our better stuff in the back and upstairs," Rusty said. "I'll be happy to show them to you when you're done, but this is a good place to start. The books are arranged alphabetically by author. A lot of them haven't been priced for a while. We notate the year that we last priced the books in the front. Anything five years old or less, I'll hold to the price in the book, but anything that has been priced longer ago than that, you have to ask me. When you're finished in here, just call and I'll show you the rest of our collection." The sound of hammering could be heard. "I'm sorry if it's a little noisy. We're having some work done."

Then, astoundingly, he left us alone.

No one had ever left us alone with books before.

The books in this first room were interesting but not exceptional and they were certainly not expensive. There was a copy of *Farewell, My Lovely* without a dust jacket for eighty-five dollars that was tempting and a copy of an 1863 abolitionist novel, *Cudjo's Cave,* notated "not a first $13."

When we were done we walked out into the hall, looking for Rusty. There was nobody there. We could still hear the hammering. It was a strange feeling to be in somebody's house, left to wander around on your own. It felt kind of like trespassing. We walked back past the staircase and got close to a tall, antique wooden country cupboard in the corner under the stairs. "Hell-o," we tried.

Rusty popped out from behind a door to the side. "All finished in the front room?" he asked.

"Yes, thank you."

"Would you like to see some of our other books?"

"Yes, please." We couldn't have been more polite if we'd been asked to afternoon tea. Actually, we felt as though we *had* been asked to afternoon tea.

Without hesitation, Rusty opened the doors to the cupboard. There were four or five shelves inside, packed with books. The shelves were so bowed from years of weight bearing that the inside of the cupboard looked like it was grinning at us.

"We have some interesting items in here," he said. He withdrew a dark clamshell box from the third shelf down. He opened it and inside was a single red volume wrapped in tissue paper. When Rusty removed the paper we saw *The Adventures of Tom Sawyer* on the cover.

There was the inevitable little slip of paper in the book. It read:

[CLEMENS, Samuel L.]. *The Adventures of Tom Sawyer.* By "Mark Twain." 8vo, original red cloth. London: Chatto & Windus, 1876. First Edition, preceding the American edition by about six months. There are some variations in the text between the English and American editions because they were printed from different manuscripts; this edition from manuscript corrected by William Dean Howells. According to the ledger books of Chatto & Windus 2000 copies were printed. Although not quite "new" this copy is certainly the finest we have ever owned or even seen. See the chapter *Tom Sawyer in England,* in Dennis Welland's *Mark Twain in England,* pp. 64–85.

There was a price listed as well; most people use that kind of money to make a down payment on a house.

Rusty took the book out of the slipcase and handed it to us. We leafed through it carefully and Rusty in no way rushed us. He stood there patiently while we looked at the book. We started to wonder if we looked wealthier than we thought we did.

We handed *Tom Sawyer* back with a mixture of regret and relief and waited to see what would come next.

He took out another big box. It contained a large, black, unmarked, leatherbound book in what appeared to be in extremely poor condition.

Rusty opened the huge old book to a page at random and we could see scribblings all over the margins.

"This book was at sea with Herman Melville when he made the notes you see here," Rusty remarked. "Then he used those notes when he was at home at Arrowhead writing *Moby-Dick.*"

Here, too, was a little slip of typewritten paper.

[MELVILLE'S COPY, Herman.] DAVENANT, Sir William. *The Works.*

Folio, later imitation black morocco (expertly rebacked, old back laid down), engraved frontispiece, pp. [8], 402, [4], 486, 111. London: Printed by T. N. for Henry Herringman, 1673.

Herman Melville's copy of the First Edition of the collected works of Davenant; signed by him on flyleaf: "Herman Melville/London, December, 1849/(New Year's Day, at sea)."

On October 11, 1849 Melville sailed for London to arrange publication of *White-Jacket.* On November 17, 1849 he bought this copy of Davenant's *Works* for 10 shillings, and evidently began reading the book on New Year's Day, 1850. On returning home in February, 1850 Melville began writing *Moby-Dick,* and the manuscript was near completion by the end of June. At p. 16 of *The Preface to Gondibert* Melville has checked the passage ". . . immense as Whales; the motion of whose vast bodies can in a peaceful calm trouble the Ocean till it boil; . . ." This passage, with "Ocean" changed to "cold body" is quoted at p. xiii in the first American edition of *Moby-Dick.*

With pencil annotations by Melville on 34 pages comprising check marks, x's, sidelines, question marks, underlinings, plus comments totaling 52 words, all illustrating passages Melville felt important such as whales, religion, monarchs and subjects, nature, knowledge, punishment of sin, etc. In one place he has written "Cogent"; in another "This admirable," and in a third he compliments Davenant "Ah Will was a Trump." The existence of this example of a source for *Moby-Dick* has been known for some time but has been "lost" since 1952.

The card listed a price that represented the down payment on a larger house but, in fact, this beat-up old volume was, we realized, priceless. It was the first item we had held since we had fallen into the book world that was truly one of a kind, utterly and completely irreplaceable, and as much a part of American history as the original of one of Thomas Jefferson's letters. Yet here we were looking at it, touching it, standing in this slightly forbidding hall, in this man's house, in an atmosphere of complete casualness. If this book had been in a museum, there would have been bulletproof glass and several guards between us and the paper.

Finally, knowing that in all likelihood we would never see this book again, we handed it back to him. "How will you feel when somebody buys this?"

"Well," said Rusty, "you know I'm a dealer. I am in business to sell books. But you do kind of regret it." He paused. "Of course,

I was lucky just to be able to have it at all. A friend of mine came up to me recently . . . another dealer . . . and said, 'I sold you that copy of *The Confessions of Nat Turner,*' . . . that's the real one from 1831, the one where Turner dictated to Thomas R. Gray while he was in prison, not the Styron novel. It was a first edition, very scarce . . . 'I wish I hadn't sold you that.' Then I said, 'I wish I hadn't sold it either.' You know you'll never see it again. Sometimes I take things with me to book fairs and, when I sell them, I say, 'Why did I take that? I didn't want to sell it.'

"A few years ago, I started to put some books away for our fiftieth anniversary catalogue . . . I wanted some really special things in it . . . I put the Melville away, actually. Then my father came and took it out and started to put it out.

" 'What are you doing with that?' I said.

" 'I can sell this. I'm going to sell it,' he said.

" 'Oh no, you're not,' I said.

"Whenever I put something away, Dad would try and take it out. I had to start hiding things in the basement."

Rusty looked over the shelves.

"I just came back from London and, if you're interested in Americana, I found something there that you might want to look at."

He removed a small, slender volume from the shelf. It was in neither a box nor a slipcase. It was unmarked except for some small printing on the spine. The covers were blue cardboard. It looked, well, cheap, like someone's extremely short self-published novel.

He handed us the book and we opened it. There was a card inside. It read:

A Complete and Accurate Account of the very important debate in the House of Commons, July 9, 1782, in which the cause of Mr. Fox's Resignation, and the great Question of American Independence came under Consideration. 8vo, modern boards, 3 p.l., pp 57. London: Sold by J. Stockale . . . at Mr. Axtell's, 1782.

$300.00

First Edition, of three the same year. Included are eigh-
teen speeches and replies including those by Fox, Burke,
Grenville, William Pitt, etc. To the debate are added the
speeches of the Duke of Richmond and Lord Shelburne
in the House of Lords on the following day, and what was
thrown out in reply by Mr. Burke, Lord John Cavendish
and Mr. Fox, in the House of Commons. Adams, *American Controversy* 82–45a. *Sabin* 15053.

"Vendors sold these on the streets," said Rusty. "That's how
people knew what happened in Parliament. If you look on the bottom of the title page, you'll see that the price was one shilling."

We leafed through the pamphlet. The pages were stiff, like
parchment, but in excellent condition and they gave off a strange,
musty odor. It smelled like history.

We had recently seen *The Madness of King George* and were, at
that moment, particularly susceptible to the debate over American
independence from the British side. It was fascinating to consider the
greater forces at work in the world at the time our Founding Fathers
were fighting for independence. That there had been numerous and
almost violent debates in Parliament on this subject was not something to which Americans give much thought. We certainly had not
covered any of this in school and we were both history majors. The
passion with which many in Britain pled for the king and the To-
ries, both on political and moral grounds, to extricate themselves from
what they considered to be a hopeless morass was startling reminiscent of Vietnam.

And as in our own Vietnam debates, it was not always the most
famous men who said the most notable things. For example, leafing
through the pamphlet, we came across this speech:

> The *Earl of Shelburne* got up again; he said, if a Whig
> was a man who acted upon Revolution principles, and was
> a friend to the constitution, and to the liberties of the peo-
> ple, he would be proud to call himself a Whig; men of

that description must necessarily be supported by the people; and such men ought of course to govern the country, because in the hands of such men the constitution would ever be held sacred. As to the American war, he had ever been as great an enemy to it as the noble Duke [the Duke of Richmond, who had spoken immediately before]; he had always contended, that it was unjust in its principle, because it militated against that great maxim of our constitution, which declares, that English subjects, in whatsoever quarter of the globe, had a right to the benefit of the British constitution, the most boasted and peculiar franchise of which was, to be governed by those laws only which they themselves had enacted, either in person or by their Representatives. That war was now at an end; no Minister could, if he were mad enough to desire it, prosecute it any longer; the revolutions of Parliament, and the general sense of the nation, were against it; and here his Lordship thought it proper to declare, in order to quiet the alarms that had been industriously raised in the minds of men, that nothing was farther from his intention than to renew the war in America; the sword was sheathed, never to be drawn there again.

His lordship's perspective was interesting. He seemed to be arguing that it was the very fact that the colonists were British subjects under the British constitution that gave them the right to declare themselves *not* British.

"Of course we take checks," said Rusty.

We were in his office, Rusty sitting at an old wooden desk, his new computer in front of him, an old manual typewriter sitting to the side. Behind him sat a very old man at his own wooden desk, which had no computer or typewriter but was, instead, littered with papers.

"This is my father, Howard Mott," said Rusty. "Dad, this is Nancy and Larry Goldstone."

We reached down and shook Howard Mott's hand. He smiled but did not get up. We had heard that he had been ill and he indeed looked quite fragile.

"It's a pleasure to meet you," we said. Rusty was entering our purchases into the computer. It seemed to occupy all his resources.

"How long have you been in this business?" we went on. Rusty looked up for a moment, just to check, it seemed, that we were not just bothering his father. He must have decided our interest was genuine because he returned to his computing.

"I got started in the thirties. I lived in New York then."

"Did you ever meet Dr. Rosenbach?"

"Oh, yes. I knew him quite well."

Dr. Abraham Simon Rosenbach, a rare-book dealer, had been a world-famous celebrity in the twenties and thirties. Rare books had done almost as well as stocks in the Roaring Twenties, mostly owing to Rosenbach, in the way the art market had exploded in the eighties. Where we had read in the paper about the astronomical price paid by Japanese investors for Van Gogh's *Irises* in the eighties, people in the twenties were reading about Dr. Rosenbach at auction in London buying *Alice in Wonderland*. We knew about him from Clarence and from that A. Edward Newton book, *The Amenities of Book-Collecting*.

"What about A. Edward Newton? Did you ever meet him?"

"Yes, certainly."

Rusty, for reasons that eluded us, after entering all of our information into his computer, now turned to the old manual typewriter to painstakingly type out an invoice. For the next fifteen minutes, Howard Mott regaled us with stories of the book world in a lost time. He was a great follower of mysteries.

"I knew Ellery Queen . . . the man who was writing under that name, I mean . . . when I lived in Brooklyn," he told us. "Not a particularly nice man. One day, a mutual acquaintance took him a short mystery and asked Ellery Queen if it had any potential. He said no. Three months later, there was the same story under Ellery Queen's name in the magazine."

Rusty had finished the invoice. We wrote out our check and shook hands. We wanted to stay and talk longer, but Howard looked tired. We promised ourselves that we would come back soon with the express purpose of sitting and listening to him.

But we never did.

Shortly afterward, we picked up the local paper and read that Howard Mott had died.

CHAPTER 13

inding in human skin? I can think of two examples," said
Brian.

We were back at Pepper and Stern, in Boston. Brian was wearing basically the same clothes we'd seen him in before: white T-shirt,
jeans rolled up at the cuffs, belt with a silver buckle, dark penny
loafers, and white socks. He was still doing his hair like a porcupine
in training.

We'd asked about human skin because when we'd received our
Bleak House from Bartfield's, Kevin had included a little thumbnail
sketch of the binder, Zaehnsdorf Ltd., taken from *The Book Collector's Vade Mecum* written by Andrew Block in 1932:

> This old-established firm has been in existence nearly
> 100 years. The founder was Joseph Zaehnsdorf (1814–86),
> who was born in Pesth, and after experience in Conti-
> nental practice came to London. He married an Irish lady,
> Anne Mahoney, in 1849, and had one son, Joseph William
> Zaehnsdorf, who succeeded him.
>
> Joseph Zaehnsdorf was a fine craftsman and speci-

mens of his work may be seen in the British Museum, and in most important libraries throughout the world . . . His son, Joseph William (1853–1930), is generally considered to have attained greater heights as a bookbinder . . . His wide experience of bookbinding brought him in contact with the great collectors of his day; his work ranged from the restoration of books damaged by fire and water to faded manuscripts; from binding a book in human skin, to one weighing only twenty-five grains when complete.

Binding in human skin had, we confess, aroused a certain natural (if perverse) curiosity and we'd called Kevin to inquire as to *whose* human skin might have been selected for such an honor. But he hadn't known. "I've seen books in zebra skins and giraffe skins," Kevin had said, "but never human skin."

"The first was *Murder in the Red Barn,*" Brian continued. "It's the true story of a particularly grisly murder where the murderer's skin was used to bind the book. I suppose they thought it would serve as an object lesson. I think it's right here in Boston, at the Atheneum. The second was much more famous. It was Eugène Sue. You know, he wrote *The Wandering Jew.* When his girlfriend—or his mistress, I'm not sure which—anyway, when she died he had one of his books bound in her skin."

"Why? Weren't they getting along?"

"Oh, yes," said Brian. "I believe they were getting along fine. In fact, I think he said that he did it so that he could always be close to her."

"Gives new meaning to the book on the bedside table."

"Quite."

It was a Tuesday afternoon in September and there was no one else in the shop. Pepper and Stern, we had discovered, was only one of three dealers that occupied the same floor on Boylston Street. The others were Thomas G. Boss Fine Books, who specialized in "Bindings, Livres d'Artistes, Books About Books, Art Deco, Art Nouveau, Arts & Crafts and The 1890's," and Lame Duck Books, who also carried first editions and had a particularly impressive collection of Latin American literature. The shelf space did not seem to be assigned in any rigorous way and wasn't marked. If you decided to buy a book, you had to ask whose it was.

As we were speaking, Brian was puttering at the desk and we were glancing over the shelves.

"Do you still have that *Tarzan*?" we asked. "The one for fifty thousand dollars?" Of all the books we had seen in all the shops, *Tarzan* was still the most expensive.

"No. It was sold. It was in California, anyway."

"Brian, can we ask you something? A dealer in the Berkshires had Herman Melville's personal copy of Sir William Davenant's *The Works,* the one he made notations in at sea and used to write *Moby-Dick.* It was thousands less. How can a copy of *Tarzan* be worth more than something like that?"

Brian shrugged. "People collect *Tarzan*."

"That's it?"

"Sure."

"Why?"

"It doesn't matter why. When something attracts collectors, they bid up the price. *Tarzan* is fifty thousand dollars because that's what someone will pay for it."

"What happens when collectors decide they're not interested in someone anymore?"

"It usually doesn't happen. Once in a while maybe, like with Galsworthy. Back in the twenties and thirties, Galsworthy used to sell for what would be thousands today. Now, nobody wants him. But mostly what happens is that interest breeds interest. Remember, with books, the supply only gets smaller. For example, who are you interested in?"

"Dos Passos? The *U.S.A.* trilogy?"

Brian nodded. "That's funny." He walked to the bookcase on the left-hand wall, withdrew a large clamshell box, and placed it on the glass case in the center of the room. "You almost never see these together," he said.

He opened the box and withdrew three volumes, *The 42nd Parallel, 1919,* and *The Big Money* and placed them side by side. "These are all first editions," said Brian.

The books were in superb condition. The dust jackets were covered in plastic and were as bright and pristine as books in a new bookstore.

"How much?" we asked.

"Twelve-fifty for the set."

Just as well, we thought.

"That's actually a very good deal," said Brian. "I've seen individual volumes go for up to seven-fifty each."

"Then why are you selling the set for twelve-fifty?"

"We price them based on what we paid for them," Brian answered. "You want to see some other things?"

There was another clamshell box on the shelf. It said *Ashenden, or: The British Agent* on the spine. "What about the Somerset Maugham?" we asked, not forgetting that we had paid twelve dollars and fifty cents for our *Ashenden.*

Brian brought it down and opened it. Inside was a copy of the book in a stunning red dust jacket with crossed lances in the center.

"How much?"

"It's also twelve-fifty."

What a coincidence. The same as ours. Only the placement of the decimal point was different.

"The dust jacket is extremely unusual. Marvelous, isn't it?"

It was.

"We have another copy, too," Brian said. "A first." He walked across the room, opened a glass cabinet, and withdrew another clamshell box. From this one, he removed another book in perfect condition. The dust jacket of this copy pictured what seemed to be the intersecting beams of searchlights. It was not as striking as the red dust jacket.

We opened the book. This copy was twenty-five hundred dollars.

"Firsts of *Ashenden* are very scarce," said Brian.

"The price of modern firsts seem to have more to do with the dust jacket than anything else. That can't be right, can it?"

"Why not?" Brian replied. "The dust jacket is the part of the book most likely to be torn or in bad condition. Sometimes a book that is not especially rare can become rare just because very few are available with a dust jacket in good condition. *The Great Gatsby,* for example. You can find a decent copy without a dust jacket for three or four hundred dollars. With a dust jacket in good condition . . ." Brian rolled his eyes.

"How much?"

"Five to six thousand, at least. Sometimes more than ten."

That explained why we hadn't found *Gatsby* at a used-book store.

"Remember also," Brian went on, "that *The Great Gatsby* was the only book I can think of where the writing was influenced by the cover. Fitzgerald was so taken by the proofs of the cover art . . . those eyes on the billboard . . . that he decided to incorporate them into the text. He even wrote a letter to the publisher insisting that, under no circumstances could they change the cover. There are people who collect books only because the dust jackets are unusual. In fact, Peter does that."

"People don't collect the way they used to," said Peter Stern, a little while later. He had joined us from his office upstairs.

Brian and Peter could not be more different. Peter was older, with a short, well-trimmed, salt-and-pepper beard, and the demeanor and wardrobe of a tenured professor. The only thing that gave away his profession was his tie, which had books on it. He had cocktail napkins to match.

"Nowadays people collect a little of this and a little of that." Peter shrugged. "They're all over the place. Collectors used to concentrate on one particular author or period or binder . . . it became almost scholarly. The collections had historic value. A private collection, even more than a university library, would be the source for serious research."

"You mean a real collector becomes almost like a biographer?"

"Well, a bibliographer anyway," said Peter. "They'll collect a specific author's papers, letters, secondary sources, like what people wrote about them, other authors who influenced them, the sources of a person's work. For example, with Steinbeck, the way his upbringing affected books like, say, *East of Eden*. If we don't get people doing this kind of thing, bibliography will become a lost art.

"There's no depth in collecting anymore," he continued. "People aren't interested in a whole body of work. Nowadays they just want the best known titles in the best condition. It's sort of like one of those remote control devices . . . always skimming the dials, never staying in one place."

We stared into the glass cabinet. Inside was a stunning array of titles. *The Big Sleep, Paths of Glory, The Hound of the Baskervilles, Light in August, As I Lay Dying, Ulysses, Gone with the Wind, Daisy Miller . . .*

"Where do you get your books? Do people die?"

"Eventually they do." He shrugged again. "I go to Ohio, Michigan, . . . all the garden spots.

"It's not like in the time of J. P. Morgan, where books were the equivalent of art. Books are not art today. In art, a person can walk into a gallery and buy a painting on impulse, just because they like it. They can take it home and hang it on the wall and tell their dinner guests, 'there's my signed Picasso.' That's hard to do with a book. You don't tell your dinner guests, here's my first-edition *Farewell to Arms*. With books you have to know something."

"Is that why modern firsts are so popular? Because with them you don't have to know anything?"

"Sure. *Catcher in the Rye, To Kill a Mockingbird, . . .* these books are recognizable, almost like art."

"So when people come over to dinner you can say, 'There's my signed *Gone with the Wind*.' "

"Or even Sue Grafton," said Peter. "There's this whole thing of hypermoderns . . . that's a field of collecting I know nothing about

. . . very, very new people who come from nowhere. Sue Grafton's first book goes for a thousand dollars."

"That's like buying penny stocks," we said.

"Worse," said Peter.

"How long have you been in the business, Peter?"

"Since 1972."

"How did you get started?"

He shrugged. "One day a bookstore needed help packing. Two years later, I went off on my own. Now here I am."

"What about you, Brian?"

"Only about a year."

"What did you do before?"

"I used to work in restaurants."

"You should see who else applied for the job," said Peter.

After Pepper and Stern, we went back to Buddenbrooks. We had been wondering for some time what was going to be in all those empty cases that we had seen on our first visit. The same dark-haired, gray-bearded, fortyish man met us at the door. Once again, he was wearing jeans and sneakers.

"Come in," he said. "Are you looking for anything in particular?"

"Actually, we'd just like to look. The last time we were here, you had just moved and there weren't any books on the shelves."

"Oh, right."

"We're Nancy and Larry Goldstone, by the way."

"Martin Weinkle," the man replied, shaking hands.

We moved into the store. Buddenbrooks is barbell-shaped. We were standing in the hallway. There were the same glass-fronted cases, each with a little lock hanging on the door.

"They look locked but they're not," said Martin. "Feel free to open them and look at the books."

We started wandering around. There was mostly English and American literature in the glass cases in the hall, sets in one room, and modern firsts in the other. The floor was covered in turquoise carpeting with Turkish and Mexican area rugs between, which set off the wooden bookshelves (and the books) nicely. National Public Radio played in the background.

The selection was incredible. We saw two different sets of Tocqueville's *Democracy in America,* both in clamshell boxes. We took one down and opened it. Inside was a piece of paper that announced that these were one of two recorded copies out of somebody's bibliography. The books themselves were so frail that they were wrapped and sealed in tissue paper, so that if you wanted to see them, you had to ask. There was an entire section devoted to rare copies of the writings by and about Winston Churchill. First editions of Mark Twain, an amazing hunting and fishing section with beautifully bound volumes, and a sterling modern-first section. Like Pepper & Stern, everything here was in superb condition.

On a table in the front were a selection of catalogues with unusual titles: "Balbriggan," "Brisance," "Ladafrium."

"What do these titles mean?" we asked.

Martin smiled. "Well, they all mean something," he said. "They're all real names. But we don't tell people what they mean, just to look them up. Sometimes we stump people. I had one catalogue entitled Atlook. An atlook is a hole in the ice through which seals surface," he explained.

"Oh."

We wandered to the back, which had richly bound sets. A pretty brown-haired woman sat at a desk with a computer near a window. "How did you get into this business, Martin?" we asked.

"Well, we were pregnant with our first child," he began.

Almost immediately, the woman behind the desk gave something very like a snort. "I love the use of the royal 'we,' " she said. "Even worse, he's talking about his first wife!"

"You're his second wife?"

"Anne," she said, smiling.

"As I was saying," said Martin, "I had to get a job. I thought I might be a stockbroker. But the day I was supposed to start, I walked into a bookstore and got a job as a clerk. In a very short time I was running my own bookstore, then several bookstores. They were new-book stores, but I got my books from every country. I went to England twice a year to buy books. And I thought I might get into rare books, so while I still owned the new-book stores, I set up a small section in the back of one of my places for modern firsts. I remember, I spent twenty-five hundred dollars on my first rare books. I was trying to get into the business. I didn't know much about it. I didn't even know the importance of a dust jacket. And the books just sat there for a while until one day a dealer walked in looking for a paperback. By chance he stumbled into the back of the store and saw my rare-book selection and bought half my stock on the spot and I said to myself: 'There's something right about this.' "

"Oh, yes," said Anne. "When Marty was just starting out, you know, he really needed books, and we were on this family trip to Florida and there was this dealer north of Miami, this old, really crotchety man. He was too cheap to put air-conditioning in his shop, so he had these great titles but most of the books were in horrible condition from the weather . . . the covers were warped or they had roaches in them, you name it.

"Anyway, Marty went in and tried to look at his stock. But every time Marty wanted to see something, the old man jumped in front of him and yelled, *'Don't touch my books!'* Then, when Marty wanted to see something it was always on the top shelf and this old man would have to laboriously roll his ladder over and hike up to the top. He'd get up there, open the cover to the book Marty wanted to see, and then say something like, 'This is a great book. I think I'll mark it up!' And then, right in front of Marty's eyes, he would reach into his pocket, pull out an eraser, erase the old price, and write in a new, higher one.

"And, then, if Marty decided he was desperate enough and would buy the book anyway and said 'Okay, I'll take it,' the man would yell, *'It's not for sale!'* and put it back on the shelf.

"Later on they got to talking about Shakespeare, and the old man jumped up on the table and starting quoting passages. When he was done, he leaned over, bug-eyed, and yelled, *'It's all in the poems!'* "

———

We left Buddenbrooks (without buying anything, thank God) and strolled around Back Bay. We found ourselves on Boylston Street in front of the main branch of the Boston Public Library.

"Hey, let's go see it. Maybe they'll even let us touch it."

"I have no intention of touching a book bound in human skin."

"I don't believe that demonstrates the proper spirit."

"Call it a flaw of character. Besides, I'm not sure this is even the Atheneum."

"Oh, this must be the right place. It's the main branch. It must be what he meant."

The main branch of the Boston Public Library was a huge, sprawling building that occupied an entire block. There was an old wing and a new wing connected by some twisting, poorly marked corridors. The main entrance to the building was in the new wing. We asked at the information booth for directions to the rare-book room.

"Oh," said an older woman with a volunteer's chipperness. "It's in the old wing on the third floor." She proceeded to give us a series of tortuous directions that, once we had taken two steps from her desk, we promptly forgot.

"Oh, we don't need directions. We'll just follow the signs."

There were, in fact, signs that indicated the way to the rare-book room. After about ten minutes, however, we realized that the signs didn't necessarily *lead* to the rare-book room.

We went as far as we could before the signs stopped and ended up in a large room where a lot of studious looking people of various ages were poring over music books. We went to the desk where a young woman sat.

"Is this the rare-book room?"

"No."

"Can you tell us how to get to the rare-book room from here?"

"May I see your library cards?"

"We don't have library cards. We're from out of town. We just wanted to see the books."

"Oh, you can't get into the rare-book room without a library card."

Pause.

"How do you get a library card?"

"Are you Massachusetts residents?"

"Yes."

"Then you can get one on the first floor of the main building."

"You mean, the new wing? Back where we first came in?"

"Yes."

We retraced our steps as closely as possible and eventually found a room off to the side of the entrance that said LIBRARY CARDS. There was a line, but it was only two people so we waited.

Ten minutes later we got to the front of the line. We showed our Massachusetts driver's licenses and we got our library cards printed out right on the spot. The technology was very impressive. But when we asked directions to the rare-book room, we got the same Byzantine instructions as the last time, so instead we made our way back to the young woman in the large room who had told us we needed the library cards in the first place.

We dutifully waved our library cards under her nose. "Now can we go to the rare-book room?"

"Oh, yes," she said with complete casualness. "It's right in there," and she pointed to a door at the far end of the room. "I'm not sure the librarian is in right now, though," she said.

"And no one can see the books without the librarian . . ."

"Yes," smiled the woman, seemingly congratulating us on our comprehension.

"When will the librarian be back?"

"I'm not sure. It shouldn't be long, though."

That was a phrase we were familiar with from visits to the pediatrician's office. Nonetheless, we decided to chance it.

We walked through the door and left the long tables, tiny lamps, and dirty linoleum behind us. The rare-book room was climate controlled, wood paneled, and outfitted with comfortable executive chairs. Locked glass cases ringed the wall. There were some books behind grilles but most of the cases were devoted to the current special exhibit, the works of Aldus Manutius. Manutius, whose real name was probably Mannucci or Manuzio, was a sixteenth-century Venetian binder who developed a new style of type called *italics,* which allowed books to be printed in pocket size and thus made written knowledge available for the first time to the general population.

In the center of the room was a desk. An older, harried-looking woman sat behind the desk and an attractive, impeccably dressed blond woman of about forty was sitting in a chair next to the desk. The impeccably dressed woman was filling out papers and was handing them to the older, harried-looking woman.

We stood at a respectful distance behind these two, waiting our turn. We looked around again and realized that the one thing missing in the rare-book room was rare books.

The older woman got up and went out of the room for a moment. The woman waiting by the desk smiled at us. We ventured a question.

"Where are the books?"

"Oh, they don't keep them out here," she said, speaking with a soft, cultured Southern accent.

"Is there another rare-book room?"

"No. This is the only one. Have you your letter of introduction?"

"Letter of introduction? What letter of introduction?"

"Oh, you can't use the rare-book room without one."

"From whom?"

"Oh, anyone will do. A department chairman or any recognized scholar."

Before we could pursue this, the older woman returned. "You may go in, now," she said, opening a door behind her which led to an inner room and addressing the woman with the Southern accent.

The woman with the Southern accent smiled at us again. "Good luck," she said, and disappeared inside.

The older woman turned to us. "May I help you?"

"Are you the librarian?"

"No," she said coldly. "I'm his secretary."

"Oh. Well, we'd like to see the book bound in human skin."

"That's at the Atheneum," she said.

"Isn't this the Atheneum?"

"No, the Atheneum is across the Common. This is the main branch."

"Oh. Can we see some of the other books, then?"

"Which other books?"

"Well, we just wanted to browse, actually."

She gave us a withering look. "There is no browsing in the rare-book room. Do you have your letter of introduction?"

So it was true. "No, we're from out of town."

"You need a letter from the chairman or a senior professor at an accredited university or a letter from another source that the librarian will accept. The rare-book collection is only for bona fide academic research."

We weren't sure, but this might have been the first time that either of us had heard the term *bona fide* used in conversation.

"And, besides, you cannot just 'go through' the rare-book collection. You must specify which books you want to see and why you want to see them."

"But if we can't browse, how will we even know what's here?"

"You have to check the card catalogue."

"Where's that?"

She looked at us. "On the first floor."

"You mean, back where we first came in?"

"Yes."

We retraced our steps one more time and walked out of the main branch of the Boston Public Library on to Boylston Street. With no credentials (and little money) we had been allowed to leaf through Herman Melville's notes at the Motts' and *A Christmas Carol* at Bartfield's. Apparently, the "public" library was the one place where the public could not see, touch, or experience rare books.

We shook our heads and went to eat paradise shrimp and sesame chicken at the Chinese restaurant that Brian had recommended.

CHAPTER 14

ow did you find us? We control our advertising very carefully."

"We looked in the Yellow Pages."

Mr. Murray nodded. "Kevvv-innn."

It was late December and we were back in Bartfield's. Once again, Bartfield's was our last stop of the day. Our first had been Madison Avenue and the Pierpont Morgan Library, where we had gone to see the annual exhibit of the original manuscript of *A Christmas Carol*.

After our first visit to Bartfield's, we had done a little research and discovered that the story surrounding the writing and production of *A Christmas Carol* was almost as interesting as the book itself.

Charles Dickens wrote at a time when writers were afforded rock star status and he was the Beatles. He hit the best-seller list at the age of twenty-one with his first book, *Sketches by "Boz,"* then followed up immediately with *The Pickwick Papers* and *Oliver Twist*. By twenty-five, he was perhaps the best known writer in the world.

Dickens's work was published in serial form ("in parts"), a com-

---

mon vehicle at the time and aimed mostly at the general population, a kind of literary miniseries. People everywhere waited breathlessly for the next installment of the latest Dickens tale. In 1841, in New York Harbor while *The Old Curiosity Shop* was running, a crowd watched a tall schooner from England being towed to the pierhead. This was before transatlantic communication when ships brought all the news from the Continent. The crowd pressed forward. Suddenly, someone on the dock yelled out breathlessly to those standing at the ship's railings, "Is Little Nell dead?" People in the English countryside who could not afford the shilling or so per installment would pitch in together, sometimes an entire village at a time, to buy a part, which was then read aloud to the group.

When Dickens himself paid his first visit to America in 1842, he was besieged with requests for interviews and inundated with invitations from towns fighting over the opportunity to afford him a public celebration. He was wined and dined in every city he visited. On his first day in Boston, after a two-week Atlantic crossing, he opened up his hotel room door at tea time to find a line of strangers stretching down the corridor, waiting patiently to come in and speak to him. He had them all in, one at a time. When he arrived in New York, New York society threw him "The Boz Ball," in which three thousand people danced quadrilles around the thirty-year-old author in a room festooned with Dickens medallions and *tableaux vivant,* groups of performers dressed and arranged to depict scenes from his novels.

Yet, incredibly, in the very next year, 1843, Dickens's career was threatened with collapse. He was in debt to his publisher, Chapman and Hall, badgered for money by relatives and, worst of all, sales of the installments of his new book, *Martin Chuzzlewit,* (part of which was an excoriating portrait of the America that had greeted him so adoringly) were going very poorly.

Depressed and agonizing over a way out, in October of 1843, while still turning out the obligatory monthly installments of *Martin Chuzzlewit,* Dickens decided to write a Christmas story to renew his reputation and make a little money. He only had six weeks to dash off a manuscript and get it to Chapman and Hall. Because time was so short, the story had obviously to be short as well, so Dickens departed from the standard monthly installment format and instead published *A Christmas Carol* as a complete novel.

Dickens gave as much thought to the manner of publication as to the content. He wanted the book itself to embody the spirit of Christmas: the red cover, those green endpapers, the eight illustrations (four in color, a big deal in those days). These were somewhat extreme requests for a man already in debt to his publisher but he was still Charles Dickens and he insisted. This was to be his salvation every bit as much as that of Ebenezer Scrooge.

For most people, an act of desperation, going double or nothing, usually results in nothing. For Charles Dickens, however, it was double and then some. The first issue of six thousand copies sold out in a matter of weeks. Subsequent issues (with the expensive green endpapers replaced) sold out as well. Even Dickens, no stranger to meteoric success and adulation, was unprepared for the phenomenon of *A Christmas Carol*.

He received letters of praise from all over England. *A Christmas Carol* was immediately adapted for the theater. The story changed the way Christmas was viewed and celebrated in England. What before had been a one-day, quiet sort of holiday became an occasion for feasting and gifts, songs and games. Christmas cards, which had never been particularly popular before, suddenly became a fixture of the holiday. It was as though Charles Dickens had taught people how to rejoice and celebrate.

That the original manuscript for *A Christmas Carol* is housed in the Morgan Library is something of a curiosity. J. P. Morgan, while perhaps the best-known book collector of all time, also remains to this day the man who comes most quickly to mind as a word association with "greed." It was as if the living Scrooge had bought the one on the page.

The library itself, a three-story building stretching from Thirty-sixth Street to Thirty-seventh Street, is stupendous in its breadth, but it was not created solely for personal gratification. Pierpont Morgan began his collection with the express aim of bringing culture to America and establishing the United States as the preeminent base of classical scholarship. The library was created to make the best written works in the world available to the best American minds.

At the time Morgan decided to undertake this effort, virtually everything that represented the best in classical culture was in Europe. Fortunately for Morgan and his library, many parts of Europe, decimated by war, were almost bankrupt and land-poor aristocrats, especially the British, were perfectly willing, even anxious, to trade art for cash.

They sold books, letters, original manuscripts, and artifacts of national icons. No one was exempt. Shakespeare, Swift, Molière, Dante, even Gutenberg Bibles made their way across the Atlantic in a wholesale migration that Americans considered a brilliant stream of acquisition and the Europeans often viewed as looting. The result was, among other things, that if a Dickensian scholar at Oxford wanted to study the original manuscript of *A Christmas Carol,* he would have to come here. It was as if an American, in order to study the original papers of Mark Twain, had to travel to Liverpool.

This was the first time we'd ever been in the Morgan Library. We walked in through the marble entranceway, which was round with a high ceiling, and paid our five-dollar admittance fee. There were several rooms to look at, including an exhibit of American political pamphlets and campaign literature from the nineteenth century entitled "From Jackson to Lincoln: Democracy and Dissent." The exhibit was filled with fascinating tidbits of Americana. For example, while it is popular in the 1990s to think that politics has never been dirtier or more personal, it was interesting to learn that in the presidential election of 1828, attacks on Andrew Jackson as an adulterer and bigamist were so scurrilous that Mrs. Jackson died a month after the election, driven to her death (according to Jackson) by the vicious and unrelenting accusations against her family.

We wandered out of the political exhibit and through the corridors and more or less stumbled upon the East Room.

The East Room is the kind of place that makes you gasp when you walk in, something you would expect to find in a castle in Europe, not in the middle of Murray Hill. In its brochure, the Pierpont Morgan Library notes that it "was designed as a Renaissance-style palazzo of formal elegance and understated grandeur." "Understated" obviously has a different meaning to some people than to others.

The East Room was huge and three stories high. Each level was ringed with highly polished cherry or mahogany bookcases emblazoned with a repeating tulip pattern. All of the cases had glass doors with fancy iron-work grids across them. There was red carpeting in front of a stone fireplace that could easily have doubled as a garage, over which hung an enormous medieval tapestry, an ornate domed ceiling, and eight-sided windows with loop-de-loops in pale green. There were no visible staircases to the second and third floors. A guard nodded to the left and told us that there were hidden circular staircases that could only be accessed through a secret compartment behind one of the bookcases at the entrance. "You can't use them," he added immediately.

The books themselves were all but invisible behind the grill-work. We could, however, make out some of the titles and realized that there was incredible repetition, sometimes as many as ten or fifteen copies of the same work, in a variety of languages. Apparently, when Pierpont Morgan wanted a book, he wanted every significant copy that was available. But what Morgan seemed to want more than anything else was the Bible. There were reputedly thirty shelves of Bibles.

There was one Bible in particular which was in a permanent glass display case as we walked in the room. It was a Gutenberg Bible. The Gutenberg Bible was the first book printed from movable type. It was produced, page by page, in about 1455 by Johannes Gutenberg, a goldsmith from Mainz, on a screw-and-lever press inspired by, of all things, a winepress, in an oil-based ink that Gutenberg invented to adhere to the typeface. Each of the 1,284 pages contains forty-two lines and about twenty-five hundred individual pieces of type, each set by hand. There are only about fifty copies in existence and Pierpont Morgan owned two of them.

The invention of movable type is not just a footnote in bibliographic history. It is one of the key turning points in the development of the modern world. Before Gutenberg, books could only be produced one at a time and were strictly the province of the Church. Anything created for the production of one book was completely inadaptable to any other. After Gutenberg, however, people could be (and almost immediately were) in the business of printing books, producing one and then resetting the type to produce something entirely different. As a result, books became less scarce and more available. And more available meant that more people read them. By the time Aldus Manutius invented his italics less than fifty years later, the demand for books had become so great that all of Europe was clamoring for everything they could get on a printed page. After Gutenberg, printed knowledge and the dissent that comes with printed knowledge had made its way, to the dismay of the Church, through every stratum of European society.

We left the East Room and took the corridor to the left. Around the corner, there, in another glass case, was what we had come to see— the original manuscript of *A Christmas Carol,* the one that Dickens had sent to Chapman and Hall to be typeset into the finished work. Afterward, when Chapman and Hall had returned the manuscript, Dickens had the pages bound in red leather and presented it as a gift to his lawyer. Morgan purchased it through a dealer from a subsequent owner just after the turn of the century.

Each year, the exhibited manuscript is opened to a different place. This year, it was turned to the page where the two forlorn children, Ignorance and Want, appear to Scrooge from under the cloak of the Ghost of Christmas Present. Even though this was, in theory, a finished copy, just this one page was replete with corrections. Words were scratched out; others were inserted; phrases were penned between lines, all in Dickens's eminently readable handwriting. At one point, when describing the children, Dickens added the word "wolfish" and changed "abject" to "prostrate."

"Why did he do that?"

"What?"

"Change 'abject' to 'prostrate'?"

"That's what writers do. They find the right word."

"Yeah, but 'abject' and 'prostrate.' Why would he change it?"

"What is this, a male thing? We change words all the time."

"But we're not Charles Dickens. I mean, was 'prostrate' better in description than 'abject'? Did it make the sentence flow more effectively? Did he agonize over the choice? Is there some great insight to be had here?"

"Oh, please."

"No. I mean it. Or what if it was just arbitrary, a matter of whim?"

"I don't know. I guess it will be just one of those great unsolved mysteries."

"Yeah, yeah. But still, I don't think I'll ever read that line again without wondering."

When we left the Morgan Library, we didn't go to Bartfield's straightaway. We decided to give Argosy another shot.

Argosy, you will remember, was the big used-book store on East Fifty-ninth Street where we couldn't see the first-edition section because the only woman who had a key did not come in on weekends. This was a Wednesday.

"Hi. Is the woman who runs the first-edition section in?"

"Oh, yes, that's Mrs. Lowry," said the receptionist with a smile. "She's right there at the desk in the back."

We looked back and, sure enough, there was a thin, very attractive, distinguished-looking woman sitting at a desk piled with papers.

"Mrs. Lowry?"

She looked up. "Yes?"

"Are you the person who runs the first-edition section?"

"Yes."

"Great. We'd like to see the books, please."

She looked at us vaguely. "I haven't had lunch yet," she said.

"Oh. Does that mean we can't see the books? We've come in from Massachusetts. We tried once before but they said you're not here on the weekends."

"That's right," she said. "I don't come in on the weekends."

"Well, we have to drive back tonight. Could you just let us in and have someone else watch us while you went to eat?"

"No, I'm afraid that's not possible."

Silence.

"I'm very hungry," she said.

Not wanting to turn and just walk out, we decided to browse in their recommended section. In the ten minutes or so that we were there, Mrs. Lowry made no move whatever to get up from her desk and get something to eat.

"Hello," said Kevin softly as he materialized from the back room on the right. "It's nice to see you again."

"We just came from the Morgan Library," we said, skipping the Argosy visit.

"Oh, yes," he said. "The *Christmas Carol* manuscript."

"Did you see it?"

"No, I didn't get a chance this year. I saw it last year. Did you know that they have an original fragment of *Aesop's Fables*? It's priceless. By the way," Kevin went on, "speaking of Dickens, we just got something I think you'd be interested in."

We followed Kevin across the floor and into the back room. Once again, he unlocked one of the bottom cabinets and withdrew a large box, larger than that which had held *A Christmas Carol*.

"This is a complete set," he said, opening the box.

Inside were a series of pamphlets with illustrated covers. *"Our Mutual Friend,"* read the one on top. It was Dickens's last completed novel, in parts, just as it had appeared at the time he wrote it.

Kevin took the pamphlets out slowly, one at a time. They were marvelous.

"These are the original parts that came out on the stands," said Kevin. "See, here are the advertisements." He opened to the back and pointed to one. "GLENFIELD STARCH," it read. "Exclusively used in the Royal Laundry." He handed us the part.

Yes, there was Lizzie Hexam, the heroine, and Eugene and Mortimer, the reluctant heroes, and Riderhood, the villain. And there was the part where Lizzie is in trouble and Mortimer might not . . . looking at the pamphlets brought it all back so strongly, as though we were reading it for the first time.

But this was more than just the content. These parts evoked their time. It was as though the bookseller's stand of 1870 London appeared before us. The crowded streets, the long skirts, the top hats, the carriages, the horses, the dirt, the smoke, the steam, the cobblestone streets . . . Dickens's London.

"How much?"

"It's twelve hundred dollars for the set," said Kevin. "That is actually an excellent price for Dickens in parts in this condition."

"Yes," we agreed. We knew, however, that it was useless to bargain.

"Will you sell this quickly?" we asked.

"Oh, yes," Kevin said. "There is quite a demand for these."

Twelve hundred dollars. Too much. We didn't even consider it. Well, we considered it a little.

As we were leaving, we noticed an open door to the left, which must have been closed before because we didn't see it on the way in and we would have. The door opened onto a cramped, narrow space squeezed between the partitions that set off the center and back rooms.

It was an office, about ten feet wide, eight feet high, and, at most, three feet deep. Each wall consisted of floor-to-ceiling shelves, broken only on one side by a small built-in desk. The desk was piled over eye-level with papers and other papers were strewn so densely over the floor that it seemed impossible that anyone could make their way through. Interspersed with the papers on the floor were perhaps ten or fifteen empty individual-size packets of potato chips or popcorn.

This office could only belong to one person.

"You may have noticed that Mr. Murray is a little eccentric," Kevin said softly.

CHAPTER 15

It was a cold, dark, dreary January Sunday in the Berkshires. Another cold, dark, dreary January Sunday in the Berkshires. After weeks of fruitless effort, we had finally been successful in securing our new high school baby-sitter, Rebecca, (lovely girl—always busy) from one to four in the afternoon. We were finally going to get to go out. The problem was, where to go?

We had been told when we moved to western Massachusetts that "you'll either love winter or you'll hate it." Well, we didn't love it and, with three precious hours at our disposal, we could not think of a thing to do. There were the movies, a Sunday matinee maybe, twelve screens at one complex, ten at another, but they were all playing variations on Sly/Schwarzenegger/Seagal blowing up a jet fighter/hijacked navy destroyer/major city, killing an enormous but indeterminate number of Arab terrorists/renegade CIA agents/psychotic modern artists. There was skiing, cross-country and downhill, but it was cold and it meant removing two inches of dust from our skis in the basement then fighting crowds on the downhill or driving over an hour to the cross-country facility, and, besides, we had discovered (subsequent to our move here, of course) that we didn't like skiing, not enough to actually go and do it anyway.

There was the languorous, romantic lunch, but the only really halfway decent place to eat lunch that we had found in the Berkshires was the Church Street Cafe, which was five minutes from our house and at which we had eaten regularly for the past six years, and at which we could be assured of being in and out in forty-five minutes and anyway we just remembered they were closed on Sundays in the winter.

There were, of course, the bookstores, but it had already been a long winter and we had been in and out of each one of them a number of times already.

By noon, we were getting desperate.

"You want to hike?"

"Are you kidding? It's fifteen degrees outside."

"Right. How about taking a drive?"

"You mean getting in the car and wandering around aimlessly until it's time to take Rebecca home?"

"Yeah. I suppose that's not a very good idea either."

Silence.

"Are there any dealers we haven't been to?"

"I don't think so. Let's look in the phone book."

We went back to the Yellow Pages and perused the now-familiar "Book Dealers—Used & Rare" section. There was a small, one-line listing that we had seen before but always passed over: "Minkoff Geo R Rowe Rd Alford," with the phone number. He hadn't even paid for his listing to be in capital letters as had John R. Sanderson and Howard S. Mott.

"What about Minkoff?"

By now, we realized that the smaller the listing in the Yellow Pages, the more expensive the books. And George Minkoff was in Alford, the toniest and most expensive town in the entire county. It wasn't even a town, really, just a series of extraordinarily expensive second homes, one right after another.

What's more, one of us had spoken with George Minkoff before. It was during the initial foray into the book world, two and a half years ago, during the search for *War and Peace*. George Minkoff's had been the voice on the telephone who had asked impatiently if we wanted Tolstoy in English or in Russian and then curtly suggested a visit to a *used*-book store. In short, we thought he was going to be old, crusty, and mean.

It was a measure of our desperation on that dull, dreary, cold Sunday afternoon in January that we called George Minkoff anyway and asked for an appointment to come and look at his books at . . . would one-thirty be convenient? A slightly reserved voice, not friendly but certainly not mean, sounding a bit surprised, replied that one-thirty would be fine.

Alford is a twenty-five-minute ride from Lenox. The drive, like the town, is both beautiful and desolate in the winter. We followed the instructions we had been given and found ourselves pulling up into the driveway of a large, two-story tan farmhouse with brown shutters, which looked to be at least one hundred years old and which had either been scrupulously maintained or scrupulously restored. There was no peeling or discolored paint on the clapboards. The shutters gleamed and hung perfectly square to the windows. No stored objects or piles of firewood cluttered the wide front porch as they did on almost every other front porch in the county. Even in the winter, under a layer of snow, the grounds seemed impeccably maintained. There were two cars in the driveway, both of which were clean, something of an anomaly in Massachusetts in the winter. The driveway had been plowed. The house looked out across the road to an open, snow-covered field backed by a wall of pine trees, the kind of scene that was featured on postcards and subtitled by glowing, chamber-of-commerce phrases like "Winter in the Berkshires."

We got out of the car. "God, I hope we're here more than fifteen minutes."

"Maybe we can go for a cup of coffee afterward."

We walked up the porch steps, pressed the buzzer next to the front door, and waited. Within a moment or two, the door swung open. A man who appeared to be in his forties, energetic and hospitable, stood in the doorway. He was on crutches, the permanent kind, not the ones you get after a skiing accident.

"Hello," we said. "We made an appointment."

"Come in," he said, maneuvering aside. He took his right hand off the handhold and, balancing expertly, reached out to shake hands. "I'm George Minkoff."

The front door opened into a large, warm, immaculately clean, post-and-beam country kitchen. In the center of the room sat a large, rough-hewn antique farm table, surrounded by four Windsor chairs. In addition to everything else you would find in a photograph in *Architectural Digest,* off to one side was the most extraordinary oven either of us had ever seen. It had two levels, at least eight doors, and was laid into a ten-foot-high brick wall. In front of the oven were piles of sealed cardboard boxes with mailing labels, all addressed to "George R. Minkoff."

"The oven was my ex-wife's idea," said George, offering us chairs and sitting down across the table. "She wanted to make bread. We used it once."

When we were all seated, George asked, "How did you come to me? Are you just up for the weekend?"

"No. We're local."

"What do you do?"

"We're writers."

"I'm working on a novel myself," he said. "A fifteen-hundred-page monster about Jamestown."

"A historical novel?"

"Oh, more than that. It's historical, social, and psychological. The American experience at the very beginning. It's very Joycean."

"How far have you gotten?"

"I'm almost finished. I'd say I have another couple of months' work."

"Jamestown? That's an interesting choice."

"The entire period was fascinating. You know, John Smith was one of the most important figures in American history and now Disney has made him a cartoon. He was only about twenty-five when Pocahantas saved him and she was only twelve. When he came to America, he had already spent five years fighting the Turks and was a hero in England."

"Is it historically accurate, your novel? Did you read the primary research?"

"Oh, yes, of course, but that's not what I'm really about. I'm like a throwback to a different time. You know, art is not supposed to be about expression anymore. It's supposed to deal with other things, like form. That's the modern theory, anyway."

"The modern theory?"

"Look. You have to have a historical perspective in order to understand what is happening in the arts today. You have to go back centuries. For example, one of the great gifts of the Moorish culture was the knowledge that what we see is reflected light. Once you have that, you have three dimensions, and once you have three dimensions, you have the Renaissance because before that everything was art as the life of Christ. Look at music. Nineteenth-century music is very different from any other music. Before that, it was all about theology. Like Bach. Bach *was* the fugue. When Bach died, Haydn was twenty-three years old. Bach was a total reactionary, but a great artist. Great art also happens at the end of an age, not just the beginning.

"From Haydn you have Mozart," George continued, "and an exploration of human sentiment. It was an exploration of how people felt, total expression, to the point where certain classic forms were forgotten or ignored. Mozart was writing for a middle class, a highly educated nonnoble class. And the middle class was always interested in how they felt. By the nineteenth century there were no patrons anymore. You *had* to have a mass audience. You had to differentiate yourself.

"Of course, they overdid it," he said. "The expression, I mean. It got overwrought and sentimental. So the twentieth century rebelled. In the twentieth century, art is about no expression. Today they write for academics," he finished, "or for a presumed mass mind, which is terrible." He put his hands on the table. "Well, shall we see the books?"

He got up and led us from the kitchen. "Who do you like to read?" he asked.

"Well, Dickens, of course, . . . Trollope . . . no specific period really . . . Dos Passos . . ."

"Wonderful writer, Dos Passos," George agreed. *"U.S.A.* is one of the great books of the twentieth century."

"Yes. And no one reads him anymore. Not in school anyway. Hemingway, but not Dos Passos. It seems unfair."

"Don't underestimate Hemingway," said George. "His style is deceptively simple, very poetic, like T. S. Eliot, but no one writes like Hemingway. It looks like it would be easy to write like Hemingway, but it isn't. You can do it for one or two lines maybe, then it becomes too difficult.

"The mind moves on images," he went on, "and not logic. Hemingway was like a great director. He knew exactly what images to use to make you feel that you were part of the scene . . . in 'The Short, Happy Life of Francis Macomber' you were there, facing a charging rhinoceros, you could feel what it was *like* to face a charging rhinoceros . . . it was brilliant. That's why people liked Hemingway. He was so different."

"Maybe. But that still doesn't explain why he survived with this titanic reputation and Dos Passos didn't."

"You have to understand," George replied. "Spokesmen have been chosen for their generations . . . Steinbeck for the depression, Hemingway for the great expatriate era, Faulkner for the South after *The Birth of a Nation* . . . and that's who everybody reads . . . and who everybody wants to buy."

"So, in other words, those writers who were chosen will remain popular while others who were just as good will disappear."

"Usually yes, but not always. Literary reputation is based on cultural factors independent of the text. The greatest cultural influence on modern literature was World War I because all the people who came back from the trenches weren't about to write nice little novels about manners and society. They'd seen moronic generals from the old school send smart people to their deaths in obviously stupid military campaigns. They wrote about it and, as a result, literature and the way people looked at literature began to change.

"The depression is another example. Scott Fitzgerald's reputation was very low before World War II. He was almost forgotten. The country was poor, people were reading Steinbeck.

"Fitzgerald came back but others didn't. Galsworthy was the perfect example of an author who was permanently killed off by the depression. Booth Tarkington is another one. They were representatives of a simpler, more ordered time."

We had passed through a large dining room into the living room. The furnishings were comfortable and tasteful. There were many objets d'art, including some very fine small paintings. A grandfather clock stood in the corner. On a small side table were arranged all sorts of antique spoons. There was not a speck of dust on any of the spoons or on the table. George led us to a large, cherry-wood cabinet.

"I had this specially made," he said.

The top of the cabinet was glass etched with a rabbit and a frog. On the bottom were two doors. On them was carved:

JANE	AUSTEN
GUSTAV	MAHLER
HERMAN	MELVILLE
EMILY	BRONTË
JOSEPH	CONRAD
BEATRIX	POTTER
BILBO	BAGGINS
LEWIS	CARROLL
FRANZ	KAFKA
LEMUEL	GULLIVER
FREDERICK	CHURCH
WILLIAM	YEATS

The sides of the cabinet were shaped as pencils. Carved on the two pencils were "2B or" and "Not 2B."

We looked in the cabinet. William Blake was there, as was Emily Dickinson, and T. S. Eliot.

"This is where I keep most of my poetry," George said. "The books are scattered all over the house. I'm more of a consultant, anyway. Mostly, I help people build libraries or find something that they're interested in."

"What sort of people?"

He smiled. "People."

From the living room, we went into a large parlor. A table with pictures of his two sons was at one end of the room and a large free-standing glass-fronted antique-looking bookcase was at the other. The books inside were beautiful, but there weren't many of them and what he had was all over the place. Conrad Aiken, James Fenimore Cooper, Charles Bukowski, Anne Sexton, Theodore Roosevelt. He had the second book ever written on the subject of hypnotism by Franz Anton Mesmer (where the word *mesmerize* obviously came from), translated into French from the German. They were all interesting books, which ordinarily we would have liked to have around the house, but we didn't have thousands of dollars to throw around. Until we saw one particular volume on the bottom shelf.

"Is the *Martin Chuzzlewit* a first?" we asked, opening the case and removing a beautiful golden brown book with gilt edging.

First edition, George told us, but not first issue. The first issue has 100£ for £100 in the illustration on the title page. "It's bound by Morrell, though," he said, "and is in first-class condition."

It was in first-class condition. It was also $650.

"We'll take it."

"Larry, are you crazy? George, do you mind if we talk for a moment?"

"Not at all."

We walked to the other side of the room. "Larry, we can't afford to buy a six-hundred-fifty-dollar book."

"Sure we can. We just won't go out to eat for a while."

"About six months."

"All right."

"You're serious."

"Yep."

"You want to spend six hundred fifty dollars on *Martin Chuzzlewit.*"

"Yep."

"Why?"

"Because if we don't, we'll always wish we had. Look, we've been doing this long enough to know that are certain things we shouldn't pass up. Dickens is one of them. It's a lot of money, sure, but we'll have something we'll treasure for the rest of our lives. How does that compare to a few dinners?"

"Maybe you're right."

"You do want it, don't you?"

"Of course I want it."

"Then let's get it."

"All right."

"And afterward we can go out to dinner to celebrate."

"You were right about the Dickens," said George, when we were back in the kitchen. "Dickens has enduring value. He may go up and down a little, but in the long haul that will be a valuable book.

"Today, the autographs that are collected, the books that are collected . . . these are the authors that the collectors read in high school. They've always remembered them, they have a fondness for them . . . of course, the people who were read in, say, the forties and fifties are different than those who are read in high school today. Then we read Steinbeck and Hemingway and Faulkner. I don't know what they read today."

We did. It comes from having a succession of high school babysitters dragging their bookbags into your living room.

"They read Margaret Atwood," we said.

George stared at us. "That's appalling," he said.

We talked awhile longer around the kitchen table before saying good-bye. It wasn't until we were back in the car and looked at the clock on the dashboard that we realized that we had spent the entire afternoon with George Minkoff and were already fifteen minutes late to go and relieve Rebecca.

CHAPTER 16

$\mathcal{T}he$ Thirty-sixth Annual New York Antiquarian Book Fair was held from April 19 to April 21, 1996, in the Seventh Regiment Armory, which occupied the entire block on the east side of Park Avenue between Sixty-seventh and Sixty-eighth Streets, a three-story stone fortress stuck in among the luxury high-rises. There was a preview on April 18 but, after Boston, we thought it prudent to wait for the real thing.

We had heard that the New York fair was different and the differences began at the door. The admission fee was ten dollars, not the usual five or six. Instead of an ordinary check room, there were young, attractive men and women wearing tuxedo shirts and black bow ties stationed at a small table outside the checkroom who called you "sir" or "ma'am" and noted with finality that they would be pleased to check your backpack for you.

Just before the entrance to the main hall was a large, glossy announcement mounted on an easel that said that Allen Ahearn would be conducting a seminar at one o'clock on Modern First Editions.

Just past the easel was an information table manned by prosperous-looking women with white hair who looked as if they lived in the apartment houses up the street. The table was heaped with free literature describing the fair, free copies of "the special New York Book Fair issue" of *AB Bookman's Weekly* ("for the specialist book world"), and announcements of future fairs, including those to be held in London and Amsterdam. The food area was in the rear, where little tables had been set up to allow participants to snack on $7.95 sandwiches of smoked turkey breast and arugula on whole grain bread and a small dish of fruit salad made with fresh blueberries, cut strawberries, and cantaloupe for five dollars. The only thing that was not different about the New York fair was the basic layout—booth upon booth in one long row after another—although even here, with 136 dealers to be accommodated, the scale was magnified.

Still, as we stood at the threshold of the main hall, it was hard to shake the feeling that, as with many things about New York, the differences were more of form (or grandiosity) than substance.

Wrong again.

First of all, it was a question of *who* was there. Pepper and Stern had a booth, of course, and so did Buddenbrooks and Howard S. Mott. The high-end New York dealers like Ursus, from above the Carlisle, and Bauman, from the lobby of the Waldorf-Astoria, were all there, too. (Although not J. N. Bartfield. Bartfield had taken a full-page ad in the brochure but Mr. Murray apparently did not make personal appearances.) But that was only the beginning. Of the 136 dealers, over twenty were from Britain and others were from France, the Netherlands, Denmark, and Spain. Among them were Quaritch and Maggs Brothers of London, legendary dealers we had only read of in places like *The Amenities of Book-Collecting*, or heard about from Clarence. On the domestic side, there were a great many California dealers, as well as others from as far away as Minnesota, Oregon, and Hawaii.

But more than the *who* was the *what*. These dealers brought with them strange and wonderful old maps and vellum books and pictures of ships. There were dealers who specialized in everything from Napoleonic history to alchemy to arts and crafts to dance rarities to Egyptology to Dr. Seuss to medieval illuminated manuscripts. They had fore-edge paintings, gastronomy, and golf; horticulture, incunabula (books printed before 1501), and landscape architecture.

We saw a 1668 first edition, first complete state, of Milton's *Paradise Lost,* the Duke of Buckingham's copy of Thomas Hobbes's *Leviathan* from 1651, a second folio of Shakespeare's *Comedies, Histories and Tragedies* from 1632, an inscribed presentation copy of Florence Nightingale's 1859 *Notes on Hospitals,* and the "rare true first edition of Lord Byron's first regularly published book *Hours of Idleness* (1807) in the original boards"—*and all of these were from just one dealer.*

Another dealer had first editions of all of Charles Dickens's work, including *A Christmas Carol,* and another had a first edition of *The Great Gatsby* in a crisp, bright dust jacket. There were first-edition *Dracula*s, both English and American. There were firsts of Sherlock Holmes, Trollope, Mark Twain, Melville, and Kipling, letters from Thomas Jefferson, George Washington, Robert E. Lee, George Patton, and Henry David Thoreau.

Everywhere we looked, there were signed copies, presentation copies, and copies with long, personal letters enclosed. And then there were the fine sets and private presses and limited editions and exhibition bindings. There were books embossed in gold and books embossed in silver and books with jewels on them. The only thing we didn't see was a Gutenberg Bible but we feel certain that somebody had one and we just missed it.

We didn't have to worry about being tempted at this fair, however. Limitations of net worth took care of that. We had never been anywhere in the book world before where so many dealers had printed up little handouts delineating acceptable means of payment. (Bank drafts and wire transfers were popular options.) At this fair, one or two thousand dollars seemed cheap. There were books for five thousand dollars and ten thousand dollars seemingly at every other booth. There was a book in one book dealer's case that cost one hundred fifty thousand dollars but we were so struck by the price that we forgot what the book was.

But it wasn't the overwhelming variety of the books being offered for sale or even their cost—it was the *condition* of those books that most amazed us. Many seemed to be the quality of museum pieces. It was astonishing to consider that books as much as two and three hundred years old could look as though they'd been bound yesterday.

We walked up and down the aisles gawking, calling "Look at this," or "Come over here," to one another. Eventually, we gravitated by habit and experience to those dealers offering modern firsts.

Here again, the selection was almost staggering in its diversity and in the quality of the books. There were pristine copies of just about everything in flawless dust jackets. Once again, we went from booth to booth, admiring what we saw and sometimes touched, until it began to slowly creep over us that something was wrong.

We couldn't put our finger on it at first but it seemed to have something to do with the overall *attitude* of the place. This wasn't like the other book fairs we'd been to and not just because of the books. The dealers behaved differently. The usual banter was missing. They were less accessible and friendly. They even dressed better. Often, they seemed to size you up to guess at your bank balance before they would even answer a question about something they had on display. They behaved more like the staffs of Christie's or Sotheby's or some snooty art gallery than people who, up until now, had always seemed to us to be doing this for love of the written word. It wasn't that we begrudged them making a living but here they almost seemed to be saying, "If you can't afford five thousand dollars for a Steinbeck, get out."

And as we wandered, we saw that, wonderful as they were, the books were part of the problem, too. There was an enormous amount of overlap. Among the modern firsts dealers, *everyone* had Steinbeck, Fitzgerald, Hemingway, and Faulkner. Raymond Chandler, James M. Cain, and Dashiell Hammett were also everywhere. There were gobs of Tarzan and more than a few Lovecrafts. Rare firsts by authors who later became famous, like *Call for the Dead* by John Le Carré, were as prevalent as if they had had hundred-thousand-copy printings. Anything in the world of modern firsts that commanded a high price was there and more than once. It seemed almost as if every single available copy of these books were at this fair.

And it wasn't as if these dealers were specializing in an author's entire body of work. *Only* the expensive stuff was here. There were three copies of *The Hamlet,* for example, one at $600, one at $1,000, and one at $1,250, but none of *The Town.* These were the first copies of *The Hamlet* that we had ever seen but we knew that *The Town* (even with a gray top edge) cost about $175. We saw at least ten copies of *Light in August,* three or four copies of *The Grapes of Wrath,* an equal number of *Of Mice and Men,* all of which were priced in the thousands, but none of, say, *The Winter of Our Discontent,* which goes for under fifty dollars, and the one copy of *The Moon Is Down* that we saw was priced at four hundred. It wasn't just *The Moon Is Down*—everything was more expensive here than we had seen anywhere else. It was not unusual to see books that ordinarily sell for hundreds to be here priced in the thousands. Had the dealers raised their prices just for this fair?

But this led to still another question: If *everyone* had them, how could these books be considered "rare," how could they command such prices? Did *only* the dealers have them? And, if every dealer knew what every other dealer had—and charged—how could one hope to sell a book for $1,250 when a competitor less than fifty feet away was selling the exact same book for less than half that?

"What books! Did you see those books? You never see books like that," said John Sanderson.

"Or for those prices," we said.

"Yes," he chuckled. "Things were very expensive there."

"A little too expensive," we said.

We were back in Massachusetts, standing once again in John Sanderson's basement. We'd come to talk about the fair. Only to talk. With uncharacteristic foresight, we hadn't even brought a check.

"Not really," he said. "The books were in extraordinary condition."

"And for that, a dealer can charge double or triple?"

The New York book fair was still bothering us. By the time
we left, the transparent commercialism had become so disturbing that,
even if we could have afforded something we wanted, we would not
have bought any of those books, books we had been looking for ever
since *War and Peace*. Of course, the fact that we *couldn't* afford anything only made it worse.

"Of course. Perfection is everything. Book collecting is about
the search for perfection, to get as close as you can to one-of-a-kind."

John had been at the fair. We'd seen him and, unlike many of
the other dealers, he had been completely natural and friendly, but
he was alone at his booth and so busy talking to customers that we
had had a chance to do little more than nod and briefly say hello.

"But everyone had the same books," we persisted. "They
couldn't all be perfect."

"Close to it. You must understand," he explained, "dealers
only bring their best copies. If they have three copies of a certain
book, they'll only bring their best to New York."

"So, for a perfect copy of a book that collectors want," we said,
"a dealer can charge . . ."

"For a perfect copy of a book that collectors want," said John
Sanderson, "a dealer can charge anything."

"And someone will buy it," we said.

"More than that," he replied. "There will be competition to
buy it."

"But didn't they know that every other dealer was going to
bring the same books they brought?"

"It doesn't matter," John replied. "There are enough big money
collectors out there. Sometimes they don't even come themselves,
they just send representatives. They don't care what they pay. They
just say, 'Get me this.' The worst thing possible for them is to pass
up a book because the price is a little too high and then find out that
they lost it to a rival collector. Don't forget, a lot of these people are
going for history. If they put together a collection with only the finest
books in the finest condition, they can give them to Yale or Harvard

and get a room or a plaque with their name on it . . . or it may even go at auction and then forever be known as 'so-and-so's' edition."

"We didn't seem to see anybody buying anything . . . was it a successful fair?"

"Oh, heavens yes. One dealer was talking about how he did seventy thousand dollars in one day. A lot of dealers said that this was their best fair ever. A lot of these dealers sell to film stars and people in the entertainment business, like John Larroquette." He smiled. "In Germany you have the big industrialists and in the Netherlands you have the chocolate barons. They are the ones who buy that vellum continental stuff. Here it's the entertainment business."

"Did *you* have a good fair?"

"It was all right. I made expenses. And that's not so easy in New York. It costs two thousand four hundred sixty-five dollars for the booth, which is more than all the other book fairs combined, and seven hundred dollars for a hotel room. So I'm thirty-three hundred dollars in the hole before I even sell a book. And my books are hundred-dollar books. I don't have thousand-dollar books," he said. "Some dealers bring four or five people with them. That's a lot of airfare from London or California, but their books are such that if they sell they'll make it back. Plus, it helps with having to go to the bathroom. I go alone to New York, so I have to beg people to watch my booth so I can go to the bathroom. But it's worth it."

"Why?"

"Well, it would be worth going just to see the books. But also, a dealer like me, working alone, gets to walk around, talk to the other dealers, see if there's anything I might not have brought with me that has a market I wasn't aware of. Also, I've had a lot of my stock for a long time. I can find out if my prices are out-of-date."

Out-of-date obviously meant too low. That led us to the big question. "Do dealers raise their prices just for the New York fair? Because they know the big money collectors will be there?"

He thought for a moment. "Some might, a little, but generally, no, I don't think so," he said. Then he grinned. It was conspiratorial, as if he was about to glance side to side to see if anyone was listening.

"I bought some golf balls while I was there and raised a couple of book prices by five or ten dollars to cover the cost. I had one book listed for one hundred forty-five dollars, why shouldn't it be one fifty?"

This wasn't what we were talking about. We decided to let John slide.

"One last thing," we said. "For a collector, isn't it a stacked deck? How can a collector ever hope to get a decent price on a book they want . . . let's say less than a perfect copy . . . if the dealers are buying up every copy in sight and all the dealers know what the others are charging?"

"Oh, you'd be surprised. If you know what it is you want and look around a little, you can often find what you're looking for at a lot less than you thought you were going to have to pay. No dealer can know everything. I made a mistake myself last year. I bought a book by Booker T. Washington for twelve dollars and sold it at a fair for one hundred twenty dollars. I was very pleased until I found out that subsequently it had sold for one thousand dollars and then two thousand dollars. And it was all because I didn't read a reference book by Allen Ahearn about writers' first books. It turned out that I had bought Booker T. Washington's first book. It didn't even look like original writing to me. It looked like an anthology. But it was in that reference book listed at a certain price and I should have known it and I didn't."

"So sometimes even a dealer can have a book at a price that's a lot less than it should be."

"I suppose that's true, if you can ever be sure of what a price 'should be.' "

For a moment, there was silence. Then, "Do you still have the Henry James?" we asked.

John thought for a moment. "Oh, you mean *The Awkward Age*? The one you were looking at last time?"

We nodded. John nodded back. He had his dealer look on again.

He raised the price, we thought. He walked around, talked to the other dealers, found out that Henry James was going for a lot more money than he was charging, and then came back to Stockbridge and raised the price.

"Yes," he said. "I believe both copies are still there." Was there a trace of a grin in the corner of his mouth? We couldn't be sure.

We made our way around the room to the nineteenth-century-literature section. There they were, two copies of *The Awkward Age*. We glanced at one another, removed the better copy from the shelf, and opened to the front endpaper. "1000 copies. 1st issue. First U.S. edition," it read. Then, "$200.00."

What a break. And we had just stopped at the cash machine before we came here.

"That book fair was about commodities," said George Minkoff. We were sitting in his living room amid his books, handmade furniture, antique spoons, and beautiful paintings.

"Commodities . . . as in pork bellies?"

"People who buy books at that fair don't know or care critically about the authors they collect," George went on. "It's the spokesman effect again—that's who everybody wants to buy and the prices reflect that."

"So, in other words, those writers who were chosen will have their books sell for substantially more than other writers of the same period who might have been just as good."

"Prices have nothing to do with literary merit," said George.

"But still, that implies that it's the culture and not the dealers that sets the prices for the books. It didn't seem that way at the book fair."

"Look," said George, "since the depression, books have been very cheap. The high point in the book world was the Kern sale . . . that's Jerome Kern . . . in 1929. After that, books went into decline. There wasn't any book you couldn't buy cheaply.

"Prices of books have been depressed, relative to the art market, for example. You could always have a great book collection for the price of a bad painting. Only now are prices evening out."

"You're saying that the prices we saw in New York were *not* artificially high?"

"No. Look, in the 1960s, you could buy a first edition of *Gulliver's Travels* for eight hundred dollars. At the book fair, there was one for forty thousand dollars. *And that's right.* You should *not* be able to purchase a first edition of one of the world's greatest books for eight hundred dollars."

"Okay. It's hard to disagree with that. But that doesn't explain what we saw at the book fair. We bought a first-edition *Martin Chuzzlewit* from you for six hundred fifty dollars, right?"

"Right."

"Printed in 1843 and bound by Morrell, an excellent binder, right?"

"Yes."

"Well, there can't be that many *Martin Chuzzlewit* first editions bound by Morrell around. Certainly not as many as a book that's only fifty years old that was printed for the mass market by an author who was already well known. So how can *The Hamlet* sell for almost twice as much as *Martin Chuzzlewit*?"

"It's the book *in its moment*," explained George. "*The Grapes of Wrath,* in its moment, was the perfect depiction of the depression, of its era. *On the Road* was the same way. Kerouac had the fifties, the beat generation. Hemingway had the post–World War I restlessness . . ."

"*Gatsby?*"

"Certainly, although I don't care much for Fitzgerald personally. I like the deep, mystical writers like Melville or Joyce. But, anyway, it's all romance. A book in its moment has romance. The book business is a romance business. Sometimes the dealer tries to build the romance but in general, for the right books, it's already there."

(George's "book in its moment" theory seemed undeniably true. Every time we perused a catalogue, we noticed that the dealer tried to add significance to things he was selling. Books were always being described as "important" or "unique," often with words like "scarce" attached. For example, in one catalogue, to describe a signed copy of *The Spy Who Came in from the Cold,* for which the dealer was asking fifteen hundred dollars, it read:

> The first edition of Le Carré's third book, the definitive Cold War novel, which brought a new level of realism to the genre of spy fiction . . . Signed copies are uncommon; signed firsts especially so; and signed firsts with contemporary signatures are nearly unheard of. A very nice copy of a landmark book.)

"So the dealers know which books have romance . . . or may be made to have romance . . . and try to drive up the prices."

"Dealers are certainly involved in making the market," George said. "But it's also the way people collect today. You get a lot of cabinet collections . . . a little of this, a little of that . . . whatever is in favor at the time, like somebody's idea of the hundred greatest books."

That's what Peter Stern had said. "And you're saying that this kind of collector is less sophisticated about prices?"

"I'm saying that dealers know their markets. Remember, you're seeing the highest end of the market at the New York Book Fair."

"Yes. We saw a copy of a first-edition *Dracula* in Peter Stern's catalogue last year for ninety-five hundred dollars. From the description it seemed to be in excellent condition, and Peter is certainly no cut-rate dealer. But then we picked up a copy of Bauman's catalogue at the fair and we saw another first-edition *Dracula* that did not seem to us to be in good condition, and that was listed at fifteen thousand dollars."

"Are you sure it wasn't the same book?" he asked with a totally straight face.

"The same book?"

"Sure. Dealers swap all the time. Look," he went on, "Bauman's set up shop in the lobby of the Waldorf-Astoria. Their location makes their market. People who come through the Waldorf and want some unusual gift or want a particular book will pay those prices."

He paused. "There's an old story about two dealers, one from Lucerne and one from Geneva. Someone asked the dealer from Geneva why the prices were so much higher there than in Lucerne. And he said, 'Because I'm not in Lucerne.'

"It's like the dealers who sell to Hollywood. Hollywood is the market today. Dealers who sell to movie stars who make fifty million dollars on a movie know that they can come into a bookshop and drop one million dollars on books, that it's petty change to them."

"Why are movie stars buying these books?"

"I don't know. Maybe they think if they have a library with great books in it people will think they are intelligent."

"So are *they* the ones driving up the prices? If a movie star buys a thousand-dollar book for five thousand dollars, won't all the other dealers rush out to their customers and say, hey, this book just sold for five thousand dollars but I can get it for you for three thousand dollars?"

George smiled. "They'd probably say twenty-five hundred."

"Which has nothing to do with the underlying value of the book. Like a spec stock."

"Look," George said, "you were on Wall Street. How many times did you see the price of a stock run up the same way?"

"There's a difference," we insisted. "If you buy a spec stock for five thousand dollars and the price doubles, minus commission, you get the full value of the stock when you turn around and sell it. If you buy a book for five thousand dollars and the price doubles and you turn around and sell it, you'll be lucky to get your original five thousand back."

"Wait a minute," George said quickly, "I would *never* advise someone to buy books to try to make money and I don't work with people who collect for that reason. I'm not a stockbroker. People who come to me want certain kinds of things in their libraries because they care about them and I tell them what might be available, what it is going to cost them, and then try and get what they want. I know what is important and what is not important, I know what is real and not real, and those are the things I try to pass along to the people I work with."

"But you don't do a lot of modern firsts," we noted.

"I've never been sure exactly what I do," said George.

"Then isn't it a stacked deck? How can you ever hope to have a decent collection if you're not enormously rich and are competing against people who don't care and just buy up everything blind?"

"Oh," said George. "I think the collector always has the advantage, because if he or she has good taste and gets good advice, he'll always come out ahead. First, he will have great books. Second, he will get great prices. And third, he or she will have a collection with the sort of books that nobody else can get."

"That sounds good but it seems a little tough to work in practice."

"Not if you're patient and pick your spots. If you're willing to pass up a book that you want because it's too expensive or not in good condition, eventually you'll find it for less money in better condition. What a collector needs most and usually has the least is self-discipline."

"Do you ever talk to other dealers about these things?"

"I never talk to *anybody* about these things," George Minkoff replied.

CHAPTER 17

*G*ood morning. Welcome to Swann's auction number 1729, modern literature, fantasy, and detective fiction . . ."

Swann Galleries, Inc., is located on the sixth floor of an older, slightly down-at-the-heels office building on Twenty-fifth Street, just east of Park Avenue South in New York City. Swann's was established in 1941 by Arthur Swann to specialize in auctioning rare books. They have since expanded into several related fields such as photographs and autographs, and today, with annual sales of six million dollars, they claim to be "the largest specialist rare book auctioneers in the United States."

We had read about Swann's in a number of places and had decided to call and ask about their auctions. After all, Helen and Michael's auction had been fun and the forty-five-dollar Brontë set was probably the best bargain we had acquired since we had begun collecting. Maybe we could get an even bigger bargain at a real auction in New York where the selection, or so we assumed, would doubtless be more extensive. We chose Swann's because we knew they specialized in books and it did not seem, from what we had read about them, that they would be as expensive (or as intimidating) as either Sotheby's or Christie's.

It turned out that Swann's held an auction almost every Thursday. In September, we called and asked for a catalogue of their next book auction and the one they sent us was for mid-October. It cost fifteen dollars, which we considered a good sign. We had ordered catalogues from the other houses as well and the one from Sotheby's had cost twenty-five dollars and the one from Christie's, forty-five.

"RARE BOOKS," read the title on the glossy cover of the Swann's catalogue, superimposed over the sepia-tinted detail of an illustration from lot 49, *The History of the River Thames,* published by John and Josiah Boydell in 1794. On the inside page it read:

Public Auction Sale 1705
THURSDAY, OCTOBER 19, 1995 AT 10:30 A.M.

RARE BOOKS

FINE PRIVATE PRESS & ILLUSTRATED BOOKS
EDMUND DULAC   ARTHUR RACKHAM
L. FRANK BAUM IN DUST JACKETS
ART BOOKS   BINDINGS   COLOR PLATE BOOKS
LITERATURE   EARLY PRINTED BOOKS   TRAVEL
NATURAL HISTORY   SCIENCE & MEDICINE

The Property of
ALFRED HOWELL
A PRIVATE INDIANA COLLECTOR
THE ESTATE OF DICK MARTIN
AND OTHERS

EXHIBITION
Saturday, October 14—10:00 A.M. to 4:00 P.M.
Monday–Wednesday, October 16–18—10:00 A.M. to 6:00 P.M.
CLOSED SUNDAY

Edmund Dulac? *We* had Edmund Dulac. He was the illustrator for our forty-five-dollar Brontë set. Maybe it was an omen.

We flipped through the pages of the catalogue until we got to lots 75–81, which were limited editions of books illustrated and signed by Dulac. They included *Stories from the Arabian Nights, The Tempest, Rubáiyát, Princess Badoura: A Tale from the Arabian Nights* (with an exhibition binding by Zaehnsdorf, another old friend). *Stories by Hans Christian Anderson, Fairy Tales of All Nations,* and Nathaniel Hawthorne's *Tanglewood Tales.* The estimated prices ranged from $400 to $1,200. Not only that, the Zaehnsdorf binding, "olive levant elegantly gilt-tooled to all-over floral design, with red morocco lettering piece on flat spine," was stunningly pictured on the inside front cover.

So the good news was that Dulac was a big deal and that we had been inadvertently clever at Michael's auction.

We leafed through the rest of the catalogue. The Dulacs were not even remotely the most expensive offerings. Most of the lots were estimated in the thousands, some of them in excess of ten thousand, including *The Birds of America* by John James Audubon, estimated at between $20,000 and $25,000 and something called The Kelmscott Chaucer for $20,000 to $30,000. Not to mention lot 162:

162. GOULD, JOHN. *Monograph of the Macropodidae, or Family of Kangaroos* [cover-title]. 30 hand-colored lithographed plates after Gould and H. C. Richter. 2 parts in one volume. Folio, 548×365 mm, modern red morocco gilt, red silk doublures and endleaves, front wrapper of second part bound in.
　　　　London: the Author, 1841–42 [20,000/25,000]

The ultimate coffee-table book.

There was virtually nothing estimated at less than five hundred dollars.

So, the bad news was that we couldn't afford Swann's, either.

It seemed, however, that while we had given up on Swann's, they had not given up on us. We were now on their mailing list. We got notices of auctions for all sorts of things: Posters, The Civil War, Nineteenth and Twentieth Century Photographs, L. Frank Baum and Related Oziana, Magic, Abraham Lincoln & His Contemporaries, Hebraica & Judaica, and then, finally, Public Auction Sale 1729, Modern Literature, Fantasy & Detective Fiction. First Editions, Signed & Inscribed Copies.

We ordered the catalogue. Another fifteen-dollar investment.

And this time, it worked out. The books listed in the catalogue were just the kind of thing we were interested in. And at prices we were interested in as well. Many books carried estimated sale prices of under a hundred dollars. But the prices were interesting on another level. *Catch-22,* for example, which we had seen at a book fair for $500, was estimated to sell for between $150 and $250. *The Thin Man,* which we had seen in Sheffield for $2,500, was estimated to go for between $600 and $900. *The 42nd Parallel,* part of Dos Passos's *U.S.A.* trilogy, which Brian had told us could go for up to $750, and which we had seen as part of the set at Pepper and Stern's for $1,250, was estimated here between $80 and $120. There was Raymond Chandler, a slew of Tarzan books, and Jack London, all at estimated prices wildly lower than we had seen at other dealers and book fairs. Even *Gone with the Wind,* for which a good clean copy of the first edition in a first-issue dust jacket can command up to $10,000 dollars, was here estimated at between $2,500 and $3,500.

Our first thought was: How can this be? Maybe the books are in terrible condition. Our second thought was: Let's go.

There was one other thing in the Swann's catalogue that had caught our attention. On the inside front cover, it noted that the current president of Swann's was a man named George Lowry. We had checked our business card file and confirmed that Judith Lowry from the first-edition room at Argosy spelled her name the same way. We wondered if they were related.

We had actually tried Argosy one last time on an earlier visit to

New York. We had gotten there early, just after they opened, well before lunch, on a weekday. It was raining.

We walked immediately to the desk at the back of the room, where Judith Lowry was seated.

"Good morning."

"Good morning," she said, looking up at us as if we had come to sell something instead of to buy something.

"Would it be possible to see the first editions this morning?"

"I'm afraid not. I have an appointment downtown to buy books. I'm leaving right away."

Veterans of Argosy that we were, we did not bother to ask if anyone else could show us the books.

"This is our third try. Is there some formal procedure that one has to go through in order to see the first editions?"

"You can try making an appointment," she said coldly.

We nodded. Then, just as an experiment, instead of leaving right away, we wandered to the back and went downstairs. We idled in the basement for about fifteen minutes. When we came back up the stairs, there was Judith Lowry, still at her desk, on the telephone, leaning back in her chair, chatting and laughing. Just from the snatches of conversation that we caught as we walked past her desk, it was clear that it was a personal call.

The preview for the auction was held for the five business days preceding the auction, closed on Sunday. We got into New York late Wednesday afternoon, dropped Emily at her grandparents (the beloved Nana and Papa, always a big plus), then raced downtown. We got to Swann's about an hour before they closed.

Swann's was essentially one big room. The books weren't laid out on tables like at the American Legion Hall; here they were on built-in bookshelves against a wall, except for ten or fifteen of the most expensive items that were in a glass case. The glass case was not locked, allowing anyone who so desired to remove and leaf through what turned out to be a pristine copy of *Gone with the Wind,* an excellent copy of *The Thin Man,* Raymond Chandler's *Lady in the*

Lake, and a first edition, first issue of *The Sun Also Rises,* which had an estimated sale price of between $2,000 and $3,000.

While a few of the books were, in fact, in poor condition, all of the imperfections seemed to us to have been accurately set down in the catalogue. The dust jacket of *The Maltese Falcon,* for example, was torn, but the catalogue read, "lacking the lower portion of the front panel, but with the falcon clearly visible" (which it was). A first American edition of *Dracula,* of which the Pepper and Stern catalogue had listed "a fine copy" for $4,000, was not in good shape, but the catalogue noted a "chip just beneath the title, tips and spine extremities rubbed," and the price was estimated at $350 to $500.

There was one item of great interest to us, because it was estimated at a much higher price than we thought it should be. *East of Eden,* which we had purchased at David and Esther's for $90, was estimated in the catalogue at between $350 to $500. In earlier, more naive times, we would have congratulated ourselves on a coup but now we just made a mental note to check and see if the first edition had more than one issue and we had the later one and didn't know it.

We spent some time at the preview checking things out and came up with a list of books on which we might actually bid. These were: *The Asphalt Jungle* by W. R. Burnett (100/150), *Good-bye, Mr. Chips* by James Hilton (100/150), *The Shuttered Room* by H. P. Lovecraft and others, an Arkham House first edition (100/150), *Parnassus on Wheels* by Christopher Morley inscribed and with Morley's bookplate on the inside cover (100/150) and the Dos Passos (80/120).

When we were done, we left Swann's, went to a terrific offbeat movie that wouldn't have come to the Berkshires until 1999, had dinner in a nice Italian restaurant, and then went back to Nana and Papa's apartment to sleep on the pull-out couch.

We were back at Swann's by ten the next morning. There were already about twenty people there, milling about, taking a last-minute look at the books. We saw instantly that they were all dealers. The vast majority were middle-aged men wearing glasses, although there was a sprinkling of younger men as well as a few middle-aged women wearing glasses. Although one man was wearing a dark conservative business suit and reading the *New York Times,* the rest were dressed in a manner we had come to view as standard dealer attire. The men wore jeans or ill-fitting khaki pants, plaid shirts, bushy beards, and there were lots of long ponytails on balding heads. The women wore loose-fitting, rumpled pants suits in drab colors, except for one woman in her sixties with bleached-blond hair who wore a red, blue, yellow, and fuschia running suit under a teal quilted jacket.

We were immediately cheered by this. While we considered it obvious why no one but a dealer would venture to the American Legion Hall in Sheffield to attend Michael and Helen's auction, we had assumed that in the middle of New York City at a place with Swann's reputation, there would be lots of private collectors. The fact that there were not explained the estimated prices.

There was a reception area to our left with a long counter and three people behind it. Thanks to Helen, we knew that, if we wanted to bid, we would have to fill something out, so we went and stood in front of the counter and, sure enough, a bearded man handed us a long, thin rectangular two-part card with a big 183 on the top and bottom sections. We filled in our mailing address and billing information on the top section and he tore that off and handed us the bottom, with our number, 183. "We bid by paddle," he said, nodding toward the card in our hands.

Five rows of folding chairs had been set up since the preview. We took our "paddle," strolled confidently over to the last row, and grabbed two seats, then watched with satisfaction as the chairs in front of us began to fill up.

A podium had been set up at the front, along with a table on which sat two telephones. After a while, a young woman went up to the podium and announced that the auction would be starting in five minutes and that the exhibition was now closed. From this point forward, she added, no one was allowed to touch the books.

No sooner had she made this announcement than the elevator door opened and a wave of new arrivals came into the room. And no sooner did these new people enter than the Swann's employees dutifully set up three additional rows of folding chairs behind ours, putting us squarely in the center of the audience.

At this point, two men who had been standing near the books by the front ambled over to the podium. One was a tall, thin, balding, well-groomed man in his fifties wearing a gray suit, a red striped shirt, and a red-and-black tie. The other was much younger, late twenties or early thirties, with close-cropped black hair, wearing a brown suit and tie. They took their places side by side at the podium. We assumed from looking in the catalogue that the older man was George Lowry and that the younger man was one of the two other licensed auctioneers, one of whom was George's son, Nicholas.

The older man addressed the audience. He was obviously to be the auctioneer. Although his demeanor was perfectly serious and professional, he seemed somehow to have a smile on his face. There was something about the ease with which he moved and the obvious enjoyment of his position that made us smile as well. In addition, we got the feeling that there was never anything that had happened or could happen at an auction house that George Lowry hadn't seen.

"We'll take a rest after item two-oh-five," he said. "That's exactly halfway. We hope you'll get up, stretch, talk to your neighbor, maybe sell a few books." So everyone there *was* a dealer. "Then we'll change auctioneers and do the second half. For those of you who haven't been with us before, we bid by paddle. If we are giving a bid that has been left with us, we will say 'by order' and we will also note if a bid is being made by telephone. We retain the right to reopen the bidding if we have missed someone, but under no circumstances will we reopen bidding once the next item has been called. Bear with me if I don't see you, that's why he's here . . . ," gesturing with his thumb to the younger man on the left, who grinned. "He can see. We will begin with lot number one, Charles Addams, *My Crowd*."

"We begin with an order bid of fifty dollars," said the younger man, looking down at something in front of him on the podium.

The Charles Addams went for eighty dollars, which was right in the middle of the estimate of 60/90.

The bidding went very fast. Often, there was no counter to the order bid, even when it was below the low figure of the estimated value. In fact, of the first twenty items, with the exception of two lots, nothing exceeded the high estimate and most went for less than the low figure on the estimated value. Only a 1911 first edition of *Zuleika Dobson* by Max Beerbohm excited any interest, going for $325 after some spirited bidding, against a high estimate of $150. A lot of three James Baldwin first editions, on the other hand, went for sixty dollars when the low figure on the estimate was a hundred.

This was very encouraging, because *The Asphalt Jungle* was next and we were hoping for a bargain. We picked up our paddle.

"Wow, this is fun."

"Item twenty-one," said the auctioneer. *"The Asphalt Jungle* by W. R. Burnett. A fine copy of the first edition with the black dust jacket."

Immediately, the man to his right said, "We begin with an order bid of one hundred thirty dollars."

We put down our paddle. Bidding increments between $100 and $150 were ten dollars and if we bid $140 and added on the 15 percent buyer's premium and sales tax, it meant paying $175 for the book. That seemed too much, especially so early in the proceedings. We didn't want to be in the position of passing up a later bargain because we had spent too much too soon. Still, by the time the next lot, *Back to the Stone Age* by Edgar Rice Burroughs, had been called, we were already regretting our inaction. We knew, now that we had passed it up, if we ever wanted *The Asphalt Jungle,* we were, in all likelihood, going to have to pay upward of $350 to a dealer in order to get it.

There were seventeen Burroughs books, the majority of them some form of Tarzan, most in the $600 to $800 range. After Pepper and Stern, we had expected these to easily exceed the high estimate but here, too, the bids were low. Most of the books went to the same two or three bidders. We realized that each of these dealers obviously had a customer who collected Burroughs and they could count on a quick turn-around and easy profit, all the quicker and easier because of the low prices.

As the bidding moved on, we were again surprised at the number of items that were taken by order bids that went uncontested. Raymond Chandler got some contested bidding although, except for *The Lady in the Lake,* which went for $1,100 against a $900 high estimate, none of the winning bids was that high. Winston Churchill did poorly, as did Joseph Conrad.

Then it was time for Dos Passos. There were eight. The first, *Airways, Inc.,* had an estimated value of $100 to $150.

"We begin with an order bid of one hundred fifty dollars," said the younger man.

Bad sign.

The bid stood and *The 42nd Parallel* was next. This time, we weren't going to bargain hunt. Even if the bidding opened in the middle of the $80 to $120 range, we were going to bid. We picked up our paddle.

"We begin with an order bid of one hundred fifty dollars," said the younger man.

"One seventy-five," immediately countered the auctioneer, indicating someone in the audience, not us. (Bidding was by $25 increments between $150 and $500.)

We put down our paddle.

"In the room," he said, "at one seventy-five. Will anyone go to two hundred. No?" He paused, then clapped the little wooden cup he was using instead of a gavel. "Sold, for one hundred seventy-five dollars, to number . . ." He read off someone's number in a row behind us.

Sigh.

Dos Passos did very well, each of the eight exceeding the high estimate, some by as much as 100 percent. It gave us some small consolation that Dos Passos seemed to be finally getting his due. It would have been a lot nicer, however, if he had gotten it at the next auction.

We sat glumly as the bidding proceeded through Conan Doyle,

Drieser, and T. S. Eliot. Then we came to lot 109, "Group of 5 First Editions" by Loren Estleman, "all warmly inscribed and signed by Estleman." Lot 110 was "Group of 9 Inscribed and Signed Volumes," also by Estleman and lot 111 was another "Group of 9 Volumes," "First Editions. All Warmly Inscribed and Signed by Estleman." Some examples of the titles were *Angel Eyes, Whiskey River, Bloody Season,* and *The Glass Highway.*

When the bidding began on the first lot (estimated to sell at between $200 and $300), the younger man on the right said, "We open with an order bid of one hundred ten dollars."

There was no sign of any stirring in the room. "Sold to order at one-ten," said the older man.

Lot 110, also valued at between $200 and $300, also went to order at $110. Lot 111 opened with an order bid of $120.

We heard a voice behind us, one of the dealers. "You really ought to buy that," he told his neighbor. "He's going to be famous one day."

"Who is he?" asked the neighbor.

"How should I know? I never heard of him," answered the dealer.

The auction went on. Faulkner did very well. Fitzgerald was a surprise. A first edition of *The Beautiful and the Damned,* with a dust jacket, estimated at $880 to $1,200, opened—and closed—with an order bid of $2,600. That number caused a murmur in the crowd. You could almost hear all the dealers frantically making notes to remind themselves to mark up all their Fitzgeralds as soon as they got back to the shop.

The Thin Man went for $2,000, more than doubling its high estimate. That meant that the copy we had seen in Sheffield was now a bargain. We sat up straighter as we got closer to James Hilton and *Good-bye, Mr. Chips.* But first, we had to go through Hemingway.

They had quite a few Hemingways but things didn't get going until lot 184.

"*The Sun Also Rises,*" announced the auctioneer. "A fine copy of the first edition."

"We begin with an order bid of fifteen hundred dollars," said the younger man.

Bidding increments between $500 and $2,000 were $100 and immediately the auctioneer said, "One thousand six hundred," then "seven . . . eight . . . one thousand nine hundred," then, "on the phone, two thousand." Over $2,000, the bidding increments jumped to $200.

"In the room, twenty-two hundred," said the auctioneer. "On the telephone in the back, twenty-four." We realized that every telephone in the room was in use, not just the two telephones at the table in the front.

"In the room, twenty-six . . . on the telephone at the front, twenty-eight . . . three thousand, in the back." The bidding was now at the high end of the range. The bidder in the room shook his head, leaving the two telephone bidders to fight it out.

"Thirty-two hundred, at the front . . . thirty-four . . . thirty-six . . ." The bidding kept on through four thousand, then five. The dealers in the room were looking at each other, shrugging and gesturing.

"Fifty-two hundred . . . fifty-four." There was a little more time between the bids now. "Fifty-six, at the back . . . fifty-eight . . ." then, after a few seconds, "six thousand dollars." The bidding increments jumped to $500 now.

"I have six-thousand dollars in the back . . ." The auctioneer looked at the woman on the telephone at the front table. "Do I hear sixty-five hundred?" There was a pause, then the woman said something to the bidder on the other end of the line.

Finally, she shook her head.

Clap! went the little wooden cup. "Sold for six thousand dollars to number . . ." The auctioneer gave the paddle number of the telephone bidder. The dealers were shaking their heads with a mixture of disbelief and greed.

"Congratulations," said the auctioneer. Then, in a lower voice, he added, "I think."

Tranquility returned to the room as two copies of *The Torrents of Spring* were sold to order bidders in the middle of their estimated values.

Then Hemingway was done and it was time for James Hilton. We picked up our paddle.

"Lot one-sixty-seven," said the auctioneer, "a first edition of *Good-bye, Mr. Chips.*"

The younger man spoke, "We have an order bid for . . ." We held our breath. "Sixty dollars."

"Seventy," said the auctioneer, nodding to someone in the second row.

We held up our paddle.

"Eighty," he said, looking our way.

We waited but there was no "ninety."

Clap. "Sold to . . ." We held up our paddle again. "One-eighty-three for eighty dollars."

Yesss!

We stayed at the auction as long as we could (even grandparental baby-sitters have their limits), until the presentation copy of *Parnassus on Wheels* that had been estimated at $100 to $150 had sold for $225. (We didn't bid on the Lovecraft either, even though it went at the middle of its $100 to $150 range.) We stayed long enough to see a red-haired woman who had arrived after intermission engage in what can only be described as a war with a telephone bidder for the twenty-three Jack London lots, almost all of which, as a result, went for more than their estimates. (The red-haired woman, who left immediately after the last London lot was done, ended up with only about six or seven books, each of which she had to fight to get, leaving her in an obviously poor humor.) Both copies of *Gone with the Wind,* as could be expected, exceeded their estimates by half.

On the way out, we stopped at the desk to pay for *Good-bye, Mr. Chips.* The same bearded man handled the checkout.

"By the way, that was George Lowry at the podium for the first half, wasn't it?"

"Yes, and Nicky is doing the second half."

"Is, by some chance, George related to the Judith Lowry from Argosy?"

"That's his wife," said the bearded man.

Back in Massachusetts, we eagerly awaited the arrival of both our book and the "prices realized, including buyer's premium" sheet that auction houses send to those who have purchased a catalogue. The sheet arrived first.

We checked lot 167 and there it was, "92." That was ours. Next we checked item 348, *East of Eden,* expecting a low number but, no, there was a "402." That meant the hammer price had been $350. We had checked with a number of dealers and there did not seem to be more than one state of the first edition of *East of Eden,* so, maybe, just this once, we had done well by ourselves after all.

Then we perused the sheet to see if there was anything else of interest and a number immediately caught our eye. Lot 325 had sold for $11,500, which meant that someone had bid $10,000 for it. It was, by $3,000, the highest bid in the entire auction. What could have gone for $10,000? We hadn't remembered anything else valued so highly. We looked up lot 325.

> 325. RUNYON, DAMON, *Guys and Dolls.* 8vo, cloth; dust jacket, couple of tiny closed tears. Fine copy. New York, 1931
>
> First edition, inscribed: "To my very dear friend and companion-in-arms, Doc Morris (one of the best,) from the author, Damon Runyon with sincere regards, September, 1931."

The price was estimated at $400 to $600.

Someone had paid $10,000 for a $500 book? It must be a misprint, we decided. Swann's had added a zero. It must have been

$1,150 or a $1,000 hammer price. Still high but at least in the realm of sanity.

Unable to resist temptation, we called Swann's and asked. "No," said the man who answered the telephone, "it wasn't a misprint. The price that appears on the sheet was correct."

"Was it an order bid?" we stammered. By a lunatic? we wanted to add.

"No," said the man. "There were two bidders."

Two lunatics? We remembered the Hemingway. "Telephone bidders?"

"No. Both of them were in the room."

"Dealers?"

"Yes. I can tell you that the winning bidder was bidding for someone else."

We hung up. It had to be collectors, two people, each with a seven-figure net worth and a Damon Runyon fetish.

Two weeks later, we were in Boston. Peter Stern, who seemed to know more about modern firsts than anyone else we had met, was the perfect person with whom to discuss the auction, particularly the stunning price of ten thousand dollars for a Damon Runyon book.

"Oh, I was the underbidder," said Peter casually.

Lucky that we hadn't had a chance to offer our lunatic theory.

CHAPTER 18

I heard a story the other dye you moight enjoy," said David. "Friend of moine was down in Atlanta at an auction. They had a lot of old law books for sale, all very noicely bound in leather, but pretty much useless being completely out of dyte. Most lawyers do things by computer these dyes loike everyone else, I guess.

"Anywye, any toime a lot of these law books came up for bids, a man in the back snatched them up. He was the only one bidding, and he got them all. He wasn't pyeing much, not over fifty cents a book, but still even that seemed too much for worthless books and my friend couldn't figure out what he wanted them for. So, after the auction was over he went over to the guy who was sitting there surrounded by all these big, heavy leatherbound books and asked him, 'Why are you buying those worthless old law books?'

"The man looked up at him. 'Worthless? They're not worthless. Watch this,' and he opened his briefcase and pulled out a stack of lybels. He took one of the books off the floor and slapped the lybel on it. 'THE COMPLETE WORKS OF WILLIAM SHAKESPEARE,' it said.

"The man grinned. 'I sell 'em by the yahd to interior desoigners in Atlanta . . . the ones redoing all those old plantytion houses with the loibraries,' he said."

It had been a while since we had been back to Berkshire Book Company. The shop was busier than during our previous visits and, other than the story, we didn't really get a chance to talk to David very much. We were just as happy, though, because we had a chance to browse. Bartfield's had been a kind of fun and Swann's had been a kind of fun but here was a different kind of fun because here we knew that anything we saw that we wanted we could have.

And there was a feeling of freshness walking around the shop that we'd missed. They'd gotten a lot of new stock, even added a room. We realized that, with all the modern firsts, we really had been seeing the same books over and over and now we had the chance to explore again. These weren't the books in their moments, maybe, but that didn't mean they weren't worth reading. Many, many excellent books fall by the wayside, either don't get the attention they deserve at the time they come out or time works on them and, like MacArthur's old soldier, they just kind of fade away. The only place you can find books like that anymore is a used-book shop like Berkshire Book Company.

We were experienced now, so we knew that there were a lot of books we were not going to find here. We were not going to find *The Great Gatsby,* we were not going to find *The Hamlet,* and we were not going to find *Dracula.* But at Berkshire Book Company, unlike at places where you would find *The Great Gatsby, The Hamlet,* or *Dracula,* you might be surprised.

"Larry, weren't you looking for *U.S.A.?*"

"Uh-huh."

"It's here."

"Where?"

"In the Ds."

"It's not the Modern Library edition, is it?"

"Yes, but it's the early one. From 1939."

Unlike later Modern Library editions, which are basically hardcover paperbacks, the 1939 Modern Library Giant edition of the

U.S.A. trilogy was well bound, sturdy, and altogether nicely done. Not a set of first editions, maybe, but then again, it didn't cost $1,250 either. It cost $10.

"Hey, this is great."

"I thought you wanted firsts."

"No. Just nice hardcovers. I didn't think you could get these in nice hardcover without buying firsts."

And that, after all, was the point. It had been all too easy to catch what Kevin at Bartfield's had called "First Edition Fever." To think that a book had no value unless it was a pristine first edition of a book that everybody else wanted. In fact, one of the things that made our library feel special to us was the variety. We loved our $700 *Bleak House* and our $650 *Martin Chuzzlewit,* but we also loved our $10 Josephine Tey, our $20 *Andersonville,* our $10 *Another Country,* our $10 *War and Peace,* and we were going to love our $10 *U.S.A.*

The more we thought about it, the more we came back to our original view. You don't really need first editions at all. They are just affectations, excuses for dealers to run up the price on you, charge you a lot of money for something that doesn't read any better than any other edition.

Still, there was that fabulous *Ashenden* at Pepper and Stern with that amazing dust jacket . . .